62

FAMOUS HOUSES

Of Charleston, South Carolina

By

Jack Leland

Edited by **Warren Ripley**

Photographs by **William A. Jordan**

Published By

The Post and Courier

PREFACE

Most of the stories of the 62 houses described in this publication were published originally in The Evening Post newspaper during 1968 and 1969. The remainder were published subsequently in The News and Courier.

They were selected at random, as examples of the hundreds of architecturally, or historically, important residences in the City of Charleston.

Following initial publication of the series in The Evening Post, many of the stories were combined into a newspaper tabloid entitled "50 Famous Houses." Some 23,000 copies of this publication were sold.

The tabloid was revised in 1978. At this time 10 stories were added, nine from the original series and one (Ashley Hall) written especially for the revised edition. This booklet was published in the present size and on a more durable paper. In this format, and entitled "60 Famous Houses," the booklet went through six printings and sold more than 60,000 copies.

Revised again in 1986 and brought up to date, the 60 stories, with two additions (16 Meeting and 87 Church), have been republished as "62 Famous Houses."

A Post and Courier Publication

51 Meeting — Music room of the Nathaniel Russell House.

Russell House Was Built By 'King Of The Yankees'

The Nathaniel Russell House at 51 Meeting St. *(see cover photograph)* is a magnificent mansion built by a Yankee merchant prince early in the 19th century.

Operated as a museum by the Historic Charleston Foundation, the Russell House is furnished in the style of the era of its construction. Located on a large, tree-lined lot on the west side of Meeting Street, it is just across from the site of the southwestern corner of the original walled city of Charles Towne.

Price's Alley, which forms the lot's southern border, once was a marshy arm of Vanderhorst Creek (now Water Street) that ran along the southern wall of the original town.

Meeting Street was just beginning to become a residential area for the more affluent people of Charleston and the Lowcountry in the 1790s. The scars of the American Revolution had healed and the city once again had taken on an air of wealth and achievement. Indigo had been replaced by long-staple Sea Island cotton as a major cash crop and the rice planta-

tions, the main source of the area's wealth, once again were at full cultivation.

Charleston had become the major port of the South Atlantic seaboard and its prosperity attracted many entrepreneurs, including Nathaniel Russell, a Rhode Islander who set up his factoring (import-export) business on The Bay, the port's principal waterfront street, now known as East Bay Street.

He was a son of a chief justice of Rhode Island and had been prominent in the import-export trade in that area before the Revolution.

Russell built a wharf and a warehouse on The Bay (now East Bay Street) and established an office and residence across the street from them. He conducted business on the lower floor and had living quarters above.

However, he was "in trade," an occupation that did not rank with the socially acceptable planter, doctor, lawyer or clergy classes in the Lowcountry plantation aristocracy.

Russell became known as the King of

the Yankees, a group of expatriate Northern businessmen who had migrated southward to Charleston in search of fortunes. he was one of the wealthiest men in the United States when he decided to construct his residence shortly after 1800. He had two daughters, neither of them candidates for beauty prizes, and legend has it that the Russell House was built as a showplace for these two marriageable females.

If this was the reason, it worked. One daughter married a scion of the Middleton family who owned Middleton Place and other rice estates and had produced a signer of the Declaration of Independence. The other daughter married an Episcopal priest who became the second Episcopal Bishop of South Carolina. Together, the girls secured the Russell family's position near the tip of the South Carolina social pyramid.

Russell's house departs from the usual Charleston "single house" pattern in that entry is from the street rather than on the garden side, and one enters a large formal entry salon. From this, the stair hall is reached. It contains what is undoubtedly Charleston's most beautiful "flying" staircase, a circular stair that gives the appearance of soaring skyward without support.

Opposite the stairs is an oval library room. To the west of the stair hall is the formal dining room that opens onto the terrace and garden. There is a set of back stairs and a rear entrance off the service rooms.

The second floor rooms, which include a formal drawing room across the front and an oval music room, have wrought-iron balconies extending over the garden. There were three major bedrooms on the third floor. There are no piazzas such as are common to most Charleston houses.

Extending to the rear is a two-story dependency wing that includes the kitchen, work rooms and servants' quarters. The house obviously was designed for gracious and comfortable living and, as Meeting Street expanded southward as a prime residential area, Russell's house rested near the hub of the city's genteel quarter.

Russell's house more than lived up to his desire to outdo the other builders of Charleston houses. The Adam style of architecture was at its peak and it had great influence on this and other houses of that era. One architectural description reads:

"The house is an excercise in ellipses. Subtle curves appear in the plans of the rooms, in the astonishing flying stair and in the balconies about the middle story. Ellipses are repeated also in the principal windows and doorways, and one frames the monogram of Nathaniel Russell in the balcony railing above the entrance."

Contrasting colors, forms and textures are brought together in the composition of the exterior of two types of brick, wood, marble and wrought iron. The use of balconies permits the tall windows to open to the floor, thus obtaining cross-ventilation without the addition of bulky porches.

French Built Houses On Church Land

On King Street between Broad and Tradd stand the French Church Houses, reminiscent of an era of small "bourgeoisie" who built outside the wall but "below the drain."

This placed them beyond the original brick and paling walls of Charles Towne but below Broad, a social factor that has more meaning now than it did then.

When the Huguenot Church decided to invest in property upon which houses could be built in return for ground rent, it went about it with typical French bourgeois prudence and methodism.

What the French would call the "triples" stand today as picturesque examples of copies of the great houses that were built farther east and south in the peninsular area. They were built around 1742 and survived the great fires, frequent hurricanes and the lone severe earthquake that have combined to do so much damage to Charleston's architectural legacy.

In a house on one of these lots, La Societe Francaise de Bienfaisance was founded in 1816. It exists today under the same name although generally referred to as the French Society. The residence at No. 98 sits on a portion of Lot 93 (actually it probably was Lot 94) of the Grand Modell of Charles Towne. The lots from No. 91 to 94 extended northward on King from Tradd with varying frontages and 254 feet depth.

The French Huguenot Church elders perpetrated what could be interpreted as one of the first subdivisions in the city. They divided the lots into narrow parcels but let them extend all the way into the center of the block. That way, the artisans and shopkeepers who rented them had room for a small garden, an item that is still the symbol of the French suburbanite.

The Huguenot Church pastor, the Rev. Francis Guichard, Gideon Faucheraud, and other leaders of the French community, signed 50-year ground rent leases on the lots. The four carved from Lot 93 (or 94, perhaps) were leased to four men. These lots — and their present numberings — went to Robert Harvey, carpenter, No. 94; James Hilliard, watchmaker, No. 96; John Vaun, carpenter, No. 98, and David Mongin, watchmaker, No. 100.

Just to the south, No. 93 was divided into two small frontage lots and a fairly large one. The men who rented them were Matthew Vanall, carpenter; Edward Scull, vintner, and William Pharrow (or Farrow), mariner.

The leases were fairly similar. James Hilliard, for instance, received a lot with a 25-foot frontage. His lease required him to build a "firm but substantial brick house" at least 15 feet wide in front and not less than 27 feet in depth with two chimneys, at least one-story tall with garrets in the roof. The house stands today, more than two centuries later, proof that

94-96-98 King — Picturesque copies of larger Charleston houses.

he built well.

Hilliard paid a yearly rental of two pounds, 13 shillings, seven pence in currency. Next door, John Vaun had a 30-foot frontage and paid three pounds four shillings in sterling.

These charming small houses are alike, yet different. They stand, narrow end to the street, guarding the privacy of the deep gardens behind, each with its own narrow carriage lane that affords all modern vehicles — except trucks — an off-street parking place.

La Society Francaise was established, according to tradition, in 98 King. In 1816 the property was occupied by Peter Fayolle, a dance teacher. At the rear of the house was a long room where Fayolle taught the popular dances of the times.

Fayolle was a follower of the Marquis de Lafayette and fought under the French nobleman during the American Revolution. Sickness prevented Fayolle from returning to France with Lafayette, a factor that probably saved his head when the Napoleons took charge. Lafayette wound up in an Austrian prison and was almost rescued by another Franco-Charlestonian,

Francis Kinloch Huger, who lived two blocks away at 34 Meeting St.

So, Fayolle stayed in Charleston and taught the young ladies and gentlemen how to maneuver around each other's feet.

When Lafayette returned to Charleston in 1825, it is quite probable that he at least looked in on Fayolle at 98 King St. because there were not many of his former French troops still in this country.

Following the Civil War, the corrupt Reconstruction and Carpet Bag leaders allowed wholesale misappropriation of property. King Street, below Broad, became almost a Negro street and gradually deteriorated, many of its houses falling apart because of misuse and abuse.

After World War I, the street began a long climb back toward respectability. No. 98, for instance, was restored by Dr. William H. Frampton in 1939.

The properties no longer belong to the Huguenot Church. Each of the surviving houses has been restored, renovated and, in some ways, changed by successive owners. Today they form a panel of beauty, examples of artisanship at its best and bourgeois living in its truest sense.

Physician Wrote S.C. History And Brought Vaccine To City

A remarkable physician, who wrote history "as it is" and introduced smallpox vaccine to Charleston, left his name on the house at 92 Broad St.

He was Dr. David Ramsay. This American surgeon in the Revolutionary War was so important to the Continental Armies that the British placed him in captivity at St. Augustine for a year after they captured Charleston in 1780. After the war, his history of the Revolution was banned in Britain because it gave detailed accounts of "British murders and villainies."

The house itself is worthy of notice without any consideration of its owner. It is a pure Georgian building built sometime before 1740. Thus it is one of the city's oldest residences.

Its downstairs living room is recognized by architects as an almost perfect example of the Georgian panel design. The builders, John Miller and John Fullerton, achieved the characteristic simplicity of moulding design around the mantel and walls and maintained throughout a perfect pattern of straight lines and round arches.

Miller and Fullerton built a number of notable houses in Charleston. In many they made discreet use of collection mouldings to dress up the austere patterns that were sometimes found during that period.

Dr. Ramsay had graduated from the University of Pennsylvania School of Medicine after studying at the College of New Jersey. In 1773, after studying under the eminent Dr. Benjamin Rush in Philadelphia, the 24-year-old doctor came to Charleston. Here he married Martha Laurens, sister of the great South Carolina revolutionist and patriot.

By 1775 Dr. Ramsay was deeply involved in the politics of the American Revolution and participated in all its stages. He was a member of the S.C. Legislature from 1776 until 1781, taking time out to serve in the field as a surgeon.

Captured when Charleston fell in 1780, he was held hostage at St. Augustine along with other prominent Charlestonians. It was during this period of enforced idleness that the energetic young physician set his mind to the matter of history.

Most of his writing at St. Augustine was from memory, but he began immediately to research and gather materials when he was liberated and returned to Charleston. Since he was elected to the Continental Congress, he literally had a front seat during the founding days of the American Republic.

His correspondence concerning historical matters included letters to and from Thomas Jefferson, Benjamin Rush, the New Hampshire historian Jeremy Belknap and the German scholar Christopher Eberling.

He finally decided to publish his first

92 Broad — Owner of house was imprisoned by the British.

history of South Carolina. It was entitled: "History of the Revolution of South Carolina from a British Colony to an Independent State." Before sending it off to Trenton, N.J., for printing, he submitted it to Gen. Nathanael Greene for reading and correction.

While giving credit where due (he praised the bravery of British Maj. Patrick Ferguson at King's Mountain) Ramsay did not hesitate to include the largely unpublicized cruelties of some British units. He particularly set down the activities of Col. Banastre Tarleton at the Waxhaws.

His history later brought about charges of plagiarism. Ramsay obviously borrowed from a publication known as the *British Annual Register*, edited by Edmund Burke, and a history of the war by William Gordon. However, Ramsay seems to have paraphrased the two publications rather than making verbatim copies.

His son, Nathaniel Ramsay, was probably the first person to receive smallpox inoculation. Dr. Ramsay also was one of the first physicians in this country to recommend that individuals boil all drinking water before use. He was one of the founders of the Charleston Museum which

originally was an adjunct of the College of Charleston.

His wife, Martha Laurens, was a woman of note. She was a patron of the noted architect, Hoban, and evidently dabbled in architecture herself. Dr. Ramsay wrote after her death in 1811 that he found in her papers "accurately drawn by her hand the first plan of the present Circular Church but without the western projection added by others. This preceded the elegant plan of the ingenuous architect Mr. (Robert) Mills and was introductory to the motion which ultimately terminated in the adoption of the circular plan." Most architectural writers believe, however, that Mills' design was primarily his own.

Ramsay continued his interest in politics after the Revolution. After serving in the Continental Congress (1782-86) he was a state senator from 1801 to 1815. He was several times president of the senate and was one of the state's most popular leaders when he was assassinated by a lunatic May 8, 1815.

His three-volume history of the United States was published posthumously. He is perhaps best known in South Carolina for a two-volume history of the state.

Broad Street House Built For Comfort

The man who brought the poinsettia to the United States lived in the house at 110 Broad St. and ate food baked in an "eye-level" oven — more than a century ago.

The house itself is an architectural museum piece that has remained virtually unchanged since its construction prior to 1728 by William Harvey.

Benjamin Harvey, a son of the builder, leased the house to Provincial Governor James Glen. Six years later, the very wealthy Ralph Izard of Goose Creek purchased it and the lot to the west. It remained in the hands of Izard's descendants until 1858 when Judge Mitchell King bought it.

Joel Roberts Poinsett, a Charlestonian who served the United States in the foreign service section of the State Department, introduced the poinsettia to this country while he was ambassador to Mexico. He married a granddaughter of Ralph Izard, Mrs. John Julius Pringle, who had inherited 110 Broad St.

They lived there and the handsome Italian marble mantels in the four principal rooms were brought by them from Italy.

The house is simply arranged with four rooms on each of three floors. These are centered around chimneys that serve both as heating adjuncts and as supports for the heavy heart-pine beams and other woodwork.

The floor to ceiling paneling is pine. It has the raised centers so popular in the early 18th century with the doors receiving somewhat more intricate carving than is normally found. Panels are of very wide planks with some of the over-mantel panels at least three feet.

On the second floor, the drawing room (east) can be paired with the smaller parlor on the west side by opening wide hinged doors connecting the two. These doors are six feet wide and are unusual in that sliding doors normally would be used in such a location.

The late John Mead Howells, internationally known architect, described the detail of the major interior doorways as unique. These are rectangular solid pine doors. However, the door framing is set inside the arched opening almost as if it were a picture frame.

The drawing room mantels are of grained white Italian marble with delicately carved figures. These include animals and a central scene in which Ceres, goddess of the harvest, is the main figure. Wooden mantels of the pre-Adam era exist in the remaining eight rooms of the main house.

A one-story, wooden, modern kitchen now connects the main house with the old "cook kitchen-wash kitchen" building at the rear. Half of this two-story building has been made into a charming small

110 Broad — House, built before 1728, is an architectural museum piece.

apartment.

The "cooking" half remains in its original state. A central chimney is about 16 feet wide. It incorporates a massive arched fireplace with a warming oven at its left. Atop the warming over and at the eye-level height so proudly promoted by modern oven manufacturers, is a quaint bake oven with an arched iron doorway. This type oven was common in the early 18th century but most of them in this area have disappeared.

When the Charleston Museum was restoring the Heyward-Washington House on Church Street, it copied the kitchen fireplace and oven at 110 Broad as part of the out-building restoration work.

The former carriage house and double stable has been converted into a residence. The wide arched carriage doorway and its flanking single-horse stable doors were made into windows. This carriage house is one of the Charleston outbuildings decorated in the Gothic style during a revival of that fashion in archictecture.

A cistern once stood above ground near

the kitchen. This large (10 by 20 feet) water reservoir filtered water into a catch basin where a wooden pump lifted it to kitchen level. The wooden pump was succeeded by an iron one that still remains as a support for ivy. The rectangular cistern hatch cover now is part of the entrance stoop to the carriage house.

No. 110 Broad is a house built both for comfort and show. Dances were held in its second floor drawing room until long after the Civil War and the layout of the house made it possible to entertain there in the grand style during the eras when Charleston was a prosperous plantation center.

Its thick brick walls serve as insulators against both heat and cold and its tremendous kitchen affords the best in cookery.

No detail was overlooked. In the northwest corner of the lot, the two "necessaries" still stand. They are of massive brick construction and, while the inner furniture has long since disappeared, in the corner of one is the remains of a miniature fireplace complete with its own tiny brick chimney.

President Of State Lived Here

South Carolina once had a president and his house, at 116 Broad St., is perhaps Charleston's finest example of a residence designed to be used for official functions.

The pre-Revolutionary mansion was the home of "Dictator John" Rutledge, president of the Republic of South Carolina, governor of the State of South Carolina, associate justice and (briefly) chief justice of the U.S. Supreme Court, chief justice of South Carolina, congressman and, by some historians, regarded as the true father of the U.S. Constitution.

And — of import — "She Crab Soup" probably was invented at 116 Broad.

The main house was built prior to the Revolution of Lowcountry or "Charleston" brick. It was redecorated in 1853 by P.H. Hammarskold, an architect who added the iron balconies, fences and stair rails. Hammarskold, acting for Thomas N. Gadsden who owned the property, added a two-story kitchen outbuilding with Gothic windows, terracotta cornices over the windows and quite unusual iron pillars flanking the rear steps to the garden.

The interior has parquetry floors and there are eight marble mantels. These were made in Europe and one of the most interesting is in the ballroom. It has carved angels, cherubs and a tiny owl, illustrating a sylvan scene.

Ironwork was by Christopher Werner, perhaps Charleston's most outstanding iron craftsman. It displays the state's palmetto tree symbol and the Federal eagle, denoting Rutledge's dual service to state and nation.

On the first floor level and from the overhanging balcony above are rods for draping bunting or hanging flags. These have brass finials and are decorated with serpents. The flag supports and the eagle and palmetto were used because John Rutledge was one of the stalwarts who molded the Province of Carolina into a state and the 13 states into a nation.

He was born in 1739, son of an ambitious physician and grandson of an Irish tavern keeper. His mother was Sarah Hext, and his boyhood was spent in a house that stood where the Heyward-Washington House now is on Church Street. He could have been born on that spot but there is no record of the exact date or location.

His father sent him to London where he studied law in the Court Temples. He began practice here in 1761, rowing home to his Christ Church parish plantation each night.

He emerged as the top man in the formation of the Republic of South Carolina and was elected its president in 1776. As such, he was commander in chief of the armed forces and saw his fledgling army triumph over the British fleet at Sullivan's Island June 28, 1776.

116 Broad — Mansion was U.S. District Courthouse after the Civil War.

His preoccupation with affairs of his state, which he held paramount, kept him from being at the Continental Congress in Philadelphia but his imprint was left on the U.S. Constitution. Years later the French writer, Alex de Toqueville, wrote that the constitution undoubtedly bore the stamp of Rutledge's thinking. The South Carolinian earlier had written his state's first constitution when it became the first republic to be established in America.

Rutledge was named to the U.S. Supreme Court in 1789 by his old friend, President George Washington. Congress refused to confirm him as chief justice in 1795 because of his outspoken opposition to the John Jay Treaty whereby Britain got the northwestern forts and American trade in the West Indies was limited. The treaty caused widespread controversy in America and further seperated Jay's Federalist Party from its opponents.

Rutledge was quite old when he was elected a representative to the S.C. General Assembly. To critics who said he was senile, supporters stated that if Rutledge had one lucid interval during a session, he could do more for the state than all other assembly members could do in an entire session.

His brother, Edward Rutledge, was a signer of the Declaration of Independence.

The house later was owned by Gen. John McPherson, one of the promoters of horse racing in South Carolina. The Gadsden family owned it for many years and it subsequently became the property of Charleston Mayor R. Goodwyn Rhett who entertained both President William Howard Taft and Mrs. George Vanderbilt there.

Although the building generally has served as a private residence, it was the U.S. District Courthouse for several years following the Civil War. During the 1950s it was cut into apartments, then served for several years as the Gaud School, in those days a private school for boys, and later, without damaging its important architectural aspects, was converted into law offices.

Charleston's "She Crab Soup" has many alleged "inventors."

One thing is certain, the soup was served at formal dinners by Mr. and Mrs. Rhett at 116 Broad St. The soup reportedly just "happened" when their butler was asked to do something to "dress up" the pale crab soup generally served. Addition of the orange-hued crab eggs not only gave color but improved the flavor, and a Charleston delicacy came into being.

7 Orange — House was constructed before 1770 of cypress and heart pine.

Georgian House Was Built In Former Orange Grove

The pre-Revolutionary mansion at 7 Orange St. was built on a lot in one of the nation's first racially integrated "subdivisions" and is one of the few private lots in the city to have a fire hydrant on it.

The big house at one time also had a servant call system based on differently toned chimes for each room. The system apparently worked, although history does not record whether prospective servants had to prove they were not tone deaf.

The bell system disappeared about the time the era of cheap servant labor died and the kitchen later was moved from the brick outbuilding at the rear into the main house. That also eliminated the need for the intricately balanced dumbwaiter that was used to bring food from the kitchen to the cypress paneled dining room.

It is a typical double house of cypress and heart pine above a stout brick basement. Its Georgian simplicity is somewhat lightened by dentils under the corona of the eave cornices, a motif repeated in the bulls-eyed pediment and pillared portico.

The land now adjacent to Orange Street was granted to John Elliott by the Lords Proprietor and achieved the epithet "Orange Garden" because of protracted efforts to establish fruit production there.

The Elliott family sold its holdings to Samuel Carne, "practitioner in physick," an Englishman who found Carolina not to his liking and returned to England. Dr. Robert Wilson, also a practitioner in "physick," and John Rose, "gentleman," acting as Carne's agents, sold the west portion of the Orange Garden to Alexander Petrie in 1747.

Petrie created a subdivision "with intent to sell to greater advantage" and left "an open street on the east side thereof of 20 feet width running from Broad to Tradd Streets for the convenience of said lots."

The lots were sold, some at public auction. One of the purchasers was "Amy, a free woman of color."

Petrie apparently built 7 Orange St. before 1770. He died that year and his will authorized sale of his "lands and houses in the town and country, Negro slaves, goods and chattels." A reference to "the new house on the property" apparently alluded to the mansion at 7 Orange.

Charles Pinckney, of the famous Carolina family, bought it from Petrie's heirs and moved his residence there from Queen Street in recognition of the growing fashionableness of the area west of King Street at that time.

Pinckney left the house to his widow; three sons, Charles Thomas Pinckney, Miles Brewton Pinckney and William Robert Pinckney; and a daughter, Mary Pinckney.

The executors were his wife, his brother-in-law, Miles Brewton; a cousin, Charles Cotesworth Pinckney; and a friend, Peter Manigault, a trio of names connoting wealth and position in Charleston and the entire English colonial empire.

Mrs. Pinckney sold the house to Mrs. Sarah Smith in 1794. It then had a succession of owners, including William Price, James R. Pringle, Mrs. Susan McPherson, E.W. Edgerton, Isaac R. Cohen, S.C. Solomons and Hortense S. Cohen, until April 2, 1913. In that year Mrs. Cohen sold the property to M. Rutledge Rivers, Charleston lawyer, educator and civic leader.

Rivers was one of the city's leading citizens in practically every phase of community life. When he died in 1940, his was one of the last of the state funerals to be held in Charleston with services being conducted at the College of Charleston of which he was a trustee.

His son, G.L. Buist Rivers, inherited the house and followed in his father's footsteps succeeding to his law practice and also serving as president of the college trustees. When he died in 1963, the property went to a son, Dr. Thomas Pinckney Rutledge Rivers, who sold the house out of the family in 1981.

The dwelling, known as the "Rivers House," took its name from this family that had owned it longer than any other. the elder Rivers permitted the city to place a fire hydrant in an alcove of the sidewalk just north of the entrance portico many years ago.

The hydrant originally was on the sidewalk, adjacent to the curb. The advent of the automobile and Orange Street's narrowness created inevitable collisions between vehicle and hydrant. This was resolved by removing the hydrant to its present position where it is safe from vehicular traffic.

The former servants' quarters and kitchen, a two-story brick building separated from the main house, became a rental unit. The attractive outbuilding was constructed of brick from Lowcountry river kilns, as were most early kitchens. This practice was necessitated after colonists discovered the tendency of slaves to burn down wooden buildings.

There are few orange trees in Charleston today, and servant bells — individually tuned or no — ring seldom. However, the solid facade of 7 Orange St., and its extensive garden area, remind one of a day when both were part of the Charleston scene.

Royalists, Indians Held Secret Meetings At Stately Residence Of British Agent

It matters not whether Francis Marion's legendary leap from a second-story drawing room occurred at 106 Tradd or elsewhere; the house has enough documented history and obvious beauty to make it one of Charleston's outstanding residences.

A Royal Stuart conducted clandestine meetings there with Catawba and Cherokee Indian leaders in pre-Revolutionary War skullduggery against the Colonists. Later, after Col. John Stuart had fled to the safety of British-occupied Florida territory, Charleston's Revolutionists conducted councils of war in the magnificent second-story drawing room of the 1772 mansion.

And that room, a beautiful Georgian-style creation, withstood the Revolution, the Civil War, the 1886 earthquake, numerous hurricanes and several tornadoes only to fall victim finally to "Yankee" gold. Today its original Siena marble mantels and ornate carvings grace an exhibit room of the Minneapolis (Minn.) Institute of Art as part of its collection of outstanding American architecture.

And when soft winds bring a damp mist in from the Ashley river marshes on a spring night, a ghostly carriage rolls up before the exquisitely ornamented door of 106 Tradd and pauses long enough to discharge a personage in 18th century costume — or so the legend goes.

Gen. Francis Marion, South Carolina's "Swamp Fox" who was famous for waging what today is called "guerrilla warfare," broke an ankle when he leaped from a window of a house on Tradd Street. Legend would have it this house but there is some evidence that it could have been a long since burned house to the west.

Anyhow, Marion's broken ankle rendered him unfit for battle, and he was recuperating at his Santee River home when Charleston fell to the British and so escaped capture to continue his hit-and-run assaults on the Redcoats.

Col. John Stuart, one of Scotland's "Royal Stuart" clan, came to Charleston in 1748, was a militia captain in 1757 and King George's Superintendent for Indian Affairs in South Carolina by 1762. He became active in the development of Florida and was a member of the East Florida Governing Council with "imperial status," being responsible only to the king.

He fled Charleston after the colonists discovered he had tried to incite the Catawba and Cherokee Indians against the Colonials. His arrest was ordered by the South Carolina Assembly, but he died in Florida. His wife and a daughter were interned in the house for a time by the Americans.

His son, Lt. Gen. Sir John Stuart, came to Charleston after the Revolution but failed in his attempt to recover the property. It was sold at auction and was held by several owners. The A.M. Lee family owned it from antebellum days until 1914

106 Tradd — Drawing room was site of Revolutionists' war councils.

when the Walter Pringle family bought it. They sold it in 1933 to John Mead Howells, New York architect, who completed restoration begun by the Pringles.

This included reproduction of the original drawing room woodwork from photographs made in Minneapolis. Howells also added the brick garden wall, replacing a wrought iron fence, and had the formal garden designed in the fashion of Le Notre, creator of the Versailles gardens. A miniature of the drawing room is owned by the Charleston Museum.* It is considered one of the most perfectly designed rooms in America and the proportions of all of the Stuart House rooms are considered models by architects.

The three-story house is built of black cypress, the "everlasting wood," with heart pine timbers and flooring. Its exact date is not known but it was before 1772. The lot on which it was built was part of an area of the city known as the Orange Garden, whence comes the name of the street flanking the east side of the house. Its carriage gates open onto Orange Street and there is a typical Charleston carriage house at the rear of the lot.

The house and gardens have been maintained in excellent condition by the various owners of the last few decades and the property today is one of the most attractive in the city.

Detail of front doorway.

*Now at Charles Towne Landing.

High Walls Discouraged Elopements

The Sword Gates at 32 Legare St. afford an opening through Charleston's highest garden wall. For down a shaded tunnel formed by an allee of tall magnolias, the old house hides its century and a half of secrets.

It has known romance — the high wall topped with broken bottles, was built to prevent elopements when it was an antebellum school for girls. The author, Hervey Allen, stayed there while teaching school in Charleston. And, as with most antique dwellings, it has a ghost.

With its magnolia-lined walk, piazzas and flower garden, it typifies the "magnolia and mint julep" image of the old South. Yet the granddaughter of Abraham Lincoln once owned it, although she never spent a night there.

For pure perserverance, the elopement that caused the high brick walls to be built is one for the annals of romance. In 1829, Maria Whaley, the 15-year-old daughter of a wealthy Edisto Island planter, caught the eye of young George F. Morris. He owned land in the parish, but, unfortunately, was a New Yorker and, as a "Yankee," was completely unacceptable to her parents. Maria's father ordered George to stay away, but the young man moved in with a family on a neighboring plantation. The neighbors were quickly persuaded by the girl's parents to refuse him lodging, so he then bought a tent and pitched camp nearby.

Papa Whaley bundled the nubile juvenile off to Madame Talvande's school on Legare Street which then had a wooden fence along the street. On one of Charleston's magnificent spring days, Miss Whaley maneuvered her voluminous skirts over the fence and married George, then sneaked back into school.

A few days later, the dashing Mr. Morris descended from his carriage at the gate and, as was the custom, sent in his card on which he had written a note saying he had come to get his wife. Madame Talvande paraded the students down the walk and this time Maria, in the suddenly acquired maturity of a matron, used the gate to join her gallant lover.

The high walls soon went up but wooden gates remained until 1849 when the house was bought by George Hopley, British consul at Charleston. He installed the wrought iron gates with sword and spear design, symbolic of civic authority since the Roman Empire era.

They are one of two sets of gates made in 1830 for the Charleston Guard House that stood on the site of the U.S. Post Office at Meeting and Broad Streets. Christopher Werner, their maker, reportedly mistook the city government's order for a "pair" of gates to mean two sets and

32 Legare — Sword Gates were made in 1830.

he was stuck with the extra pair for 20 years until the wealthy Hopley came on the scene.

It was Hopley who created the magnificent ballroom in the brick portion of the house, utilizing space that had been used as a classroom by the Talvandes. The heart pine floor planking runs the full length of the room and magnificent mirrors, installed by Hopley, afford a floor-to-ceiling reflection today. Hopley also built the northeast room on the southern (wooden) portion of the great house. This was a game room and the scene of much gentlemanly gaming at billiards, cards and dice.

The property originally consisted of two lots on the Grand Modell of Charles Towne as surveyed in 1694 and granted to James LaRoche and James Lardent, both French Huguenots. The Soloman Legare family, also Huguenot, owned the lots for many years. The house, half brick and half frame, possibly was built by these owners.

A plat of the property drawn in 1818 shows the main house and the carriage house on Tradd Street. Andre Talvande and his mother, Madame Rose Talvande, bought the property a year later. The Talvandes were among those Santo Domingon French families lucky enough to escape the bloody massacre of white planters by Negro slaves in the revolution of 1793. Being well educated, they established a school which became quite fash-

ionable, and set the scene for the elopement.

Hopley sold to the Adger family in 1853 and it was Robert Adger who replaced the sweet orange hedges along the walk with magnolias. Col. Charles Simonton, later Federal judge of Charleston, purchased the house from Adger in 1878.

Mrs. Jessie Lincoln Randolph, daughter of Robert Todd Lincoln and the last of President Abraham Lincoln's descendants to bear the family name, bought the house in 1930. She never lived in it and it had been vacant for a number of years when purchased in 1949 by Henry T. Gaud, Charleston lawyer, who restored the main house and created four rental units in the former carriage house and servants' quarters.

Gaud opened the house to tourists for a number of years and then subdivided the property into four sections in 1959.

The main house also was divided by closing the hall between the wooden and brick sections. The two units in the subdivided main house have passed through several owners since then.

Today the two original city lots contain three large residences and three apartments. But, despite the passage of years, the Sword Gates remain the same and occasionally in spring, night herons roost in the tall magnolias near the old house behind its wall that was built too late to thwart the flame of love.

31 Legare — Residence resembles town houses found in inland sections of South Carolina.

Pensive Ghost Liked Sunlight

The house at 31 Legare St. played a role in the preservation of South Carolina's Negro spirituals and one of its earlier owners was a member of the Confederate Army "Air Force."

It also has a ghost, a young veteran who was killed in a hunting accident shortly after the end of the Revolutionary War. The ghost story holds, however, only if the house can be documented as of pre-Revolutionary construction.

Its building date is generally given as 1789. However, there are indications that the main body of the building predates the conflict that tore South Carolina — somewhat unwillingly — away from its motherland, Great Britain.

The handsome residence is not a "typical" Charleston house at all, favoring rather the town house that developed farther inland. This factor is said to have endeared it to one of its owners who grew up in Columbia during the antebellum era before the state capital's beautiful homes were burned during the Civil War.

Augustin T. Smythe acquired the dwelling, probably in 1868. During the Civil War, Smythe was selected to accompany Capt. Joseph Manigault as his "best man" in an ascent in a gas-filled silk balloon to spot the Federal gunboats blockading the port.

Just who filled that particular balloon with gas is not known, but Count Ferdinand von Zepplin, who later designed the famous German airships, was in Charleston during the siege and wrote later (1929) of assisting with the filling of balloons for the Confederate aerial experiments.

At any rate, the balloon carrying Lt. Smythe burst, bringing that particular attempt at aerial warfare to a crashing end. Lt. Smythe survived the accident, and the war, and his descendants have lived in 31 Legare ever since.

The house was one of many fine plantation and town houses built by the distinguished Heyward family of Carolina. Its design incorporates the best of several plans and its huge curved "bows" at the southern and northern ends give light and distinction to very handsome rooms.

The house retains its large original lot, making it one of the downtown area's largest single residential sites. Children of the area for many years enjoyed its tennis court, now reverted to garden, and some of its palmetto trees are among the tallest in the state.

The ghost of young James Heyward may be one of the most tragic and quietest spooks on record. He survived the Revolution only to be killed by gunshot during a deer hunt after the war.

This talented young man, known as a deep thinker, was killed about 8 a.m. and at the very moment of his death, his mother reportedly walked into the handsome library of the 31 Legare St. property and saw the dim outline of her son seated in a chair, head-on-hand, in a pensive pose.

The ghost has not been seen for many years, but it always appeared on bright sunny summer mornings, always in the same position.

One of the Smythe descendants was for many years president of the Society for the Preservation of Spirituals. Many of the earlier rehearsals of the Society were held at 31 Legare St. The Society was founded by descendants of plantation owners, and former plantation owners who had moved to the city, who gathered to sing the old songs that they had heard the Negroes sing in the country.

They were asked to sing at a charitable affair one year in the early 1920s and were so popular that the Society took formal shape. It has performed ever since and is generally credited with having preserved the true Negro spiritual in this area, songs that otherwise would have disappeared.

Massive House Built About 1843

No. 21 Legare St. is a massive house, reflecting the oversized items of its era (c. 1843) — large furniture, huge families, billowing hoopskirts and the St. Bernard dogs that were the rage.

But more than that, this handsome residence is an example of the severely correct classical mansion of the wealthy Charlestonian of that time. It was built in perfect attunement with the breezes that then reached it easily across the marshes of the Ashley River to the southwest, and its piazza-end screening walls gave it privacy from Legare Street passersby.

From the Flemish bond bricklaying in its facade to the balustrade atop its stuccoed parapet, the house bespeaks the wealth of its owner and the good architectural taste of its builder. Who he was is not clear but the similarity of architectural schematism in the design of this house and others known to have been the work of Edward Brickwell White is obvious. The house either was designed by White or by someone who drew heavily on his genius.

Viewed head on, the house appears to be an unusually wide variety of the Charleston residence but the windows on the south are at the end of wide verandahs. The windows on the south and a wide entrance and stair hall on the north, flank the major rooms that run en suite between. Both the piazzas and the stair hall ends are recessed slightly form the main facade on the street.

The facade brick are laid in Flemish bond while those on the side and rear walls and the outbuildings are in running bond. The builders laid three rows of stretcher bricks to each row of headers instead of the usual five-one system. The three-to-one plan makes for a stronger wall and also costs more.

No. 21 Legare has two entrance driveways. One serves the garden at the front of the house. The other, which is shared with 23 Legare St., is along the north wall.

In order to avoid damage from vehicles entering the premises, the lower part of a corner of the kitchen building was rounded off. The upper floor was left square and this differentiation, plus a reinforcing stone slab, gives a quaint look to a utilitarian building.

The Legare Street end of the house is decorated with brownstone trim on the basement windows and door while the windows on the upper floors have marble trim, those of the second (main) floor being quite elaborate marble enframements.

An interesting architectural trick used in this house was to have the mortar tinted the same color as the brick. While the seal is pointed, the unanimity of color pulls the broad planes of the work together in

21 Legare — Severely correct classical mansion reflects taste of builder.

homogenous friendliness.

The house has a very wide staircase and the windows are furnished with interior shutters that have come back into vogue recently. The major rooms have lofty ceilings and decorative plaster work.

The porches are unusual because of their great width and the window-bearing screening walls at the street end. The colonnades are of massive columns, an architectural detail that was called for by the wide spacing of supports. Extra large plinths were used, and the columns of the main floor porch are set on square pedestals the height of the balustrades.

The lot was sold to a Virginian, William C. Gatewood, in 1843 by Edward Frost for $2,400, and the house was begun shortly thereafter. Gatewood was a factor (wholesale merchant) here who owned considerable real estate in the city.

Gatewood live here until 1863 when the house changed hands twice in a single year. Gatewood sold it to William Hart who transferred it a few months later to James H. Baggett. Each transaction was for $27,000, probably in Confederate States currency.

In settlement of a debt, Baggett sold the house in 1867 to Winthrop B. Williams, a member of the well-known Williams family of Rhode Island whose southern branch married into the Middleton clan of South

Carolina. It was occupied by the Williams family for 14 years and contained New England, Charleston and English heirloom furniture that now graces the homes of that family's descendants here and elsewhere.

The Baggett-Williams property deed specifically mentions mirrors and gaslight fixtures, indicating they had a high value.

The Williams family sold the house to Lavinia R. Inglesby in 1881. During the residency of the Inglesby family, the second-floor drawing rooms were the scenes of many parties and balls long remembered by the young people who attended them.

The Shingler family purchased the house in 1901 from Thomas S. Inglesby and held possession until 1927 when the house was bought by Rees Hawkins for $16,000. The Hawkins family sold it in 1942 for $8,000 to Joseph Miserindino, Charleston businessman. A year later it was purchased by Mrs. Henry Deas, wife of a Charleston physician.

She leased it to Mrs. Samuel J. Beckley who operated it as an apartment and rooming house during World War II. It continued as an apartment house until 1959 when it was purchased by Mr. and Mrs. Andrew Drury who renovated and restored it to a single-family dwelling.

Legare Street Residence Housed British Officers

The house at 15 Legare St. is a light and airy Charleston single house and, as such, not too much in keeping with the dour rigidity associated with Scotland, whence came the builder.

Nevertheless, John Fullerton gave Charleston at least four grand houses, each distincitve in its own right. The others are 39 Meeting, and 92 and 117 Broad St. The latter has been much altered from Fullerton's original plan for a stately double house.

A compliment to the Legare Street house was the fact that it was selected to house staff officers when the British Army occupied Charleston from 1780 until 1782. Fullerton was already dead, but his corpse must have turned in its grave at the thought of one of his houses occupied by the Redcoats.

Fullerton was a fiery revolutionist with a deeply rooted Scottish hatred of the British. He was one of Charleston's Whigs who were led by Christopher Gadsden and held their meetings under the "Liberty Tree," a giant liveoak in Mazyck's Pasture near Alexander and Charlotte Streets.

The British took the precaution of cutting the tree down, digging up its roots and burning the whole bit in an attempt to destroy a rallying symbol of the revolutionary patriots.

The house had been built by the Scot of native brick, pine and cypress, and it is a happy monument to the good taste and accomplished workmanship of the man.

Among the things that mark Fullerton's attention for detail are the window casings, especially those of the first two floors. His acquaintance with Renaissance tradition is evidenced in these casings known as "tabernacle frames" in Fullerton's day. He scaled down the wooden casings to suit the windows he planned, copying the details "in miniature" from designs found in Roman palaces.

The casings are practically perfect from the consoles supporting the bottom sills to the pediments capping the decorative pieces near the ceiling.

The house apparently was built before 1777. In that year Fullerton and his wife, Elizabeth, sold the southern 45-foot frontage of an 80-foot lot for 4,700 pounds, indicating that a substantial house was on the property.

Fullerton apparently bought a tract of land on lower Legare Street (then Johnson Street) in 1772 from William Gibbes. The tract was called "White Point" in the deed and it is not explained whether this was the name generally applied to all of the old peninsula or simply to that portion of it. Today the term "White Point" continues only in the park at the southern tip of the peninsula. Fullerton paid 5,600 pounds for the entire area and apparently sold most of it as building lots.

The property at 15 Legare was owned successively by George Cooke, David

Ornamental window casings.

Campbell, Thomas Lowndes and Margaret Stock before 1806 when it received its first long-term owner, Micah Jenkins of the Edisto Island plantation clan.

The Jenkins family held it until 1831 when it was sold to Paul Trapier Gervais. He disposed of it quickly to Elizabeth St. J. Ball who sold it to Charlotte W. Smith in 1837 for $10,000. That price was consistent with the rice and cotton prosperity of Charleston, not yet ruined by the Civil War. When Mary A. Wragg bought it in 1884, the city was still rebuilding from the war. The state was destitute, and she paid only $5,000 for the property.

When her will was probated in 1926, Robert S. Manigault bought the house, paying $22,000 for it.

The second floor rooms are divided by ingenuously contrived folding doors that may be recessed to create a large ballroom. It was from a third floor window of this house that a member of the Lowndes family engaged in a duel with a kinsman occupying a similar bedroom position in 14 Legare, just across the street. The duelest in 15 was unscathed but his cousin across the street suffered a fatal pistol ball wound.

During the British occupation of Charleston, officers on the staffs of Generals Cornwallis and Clinton were housed in No. 15. The generals lived in the Miles Brewton House at 27 King St., just a block to the east. There were no buildings on the lots across Legare Street at that time and the junior officers commuted to headquarters through a postern gate at the rear of the Brewton House grounds.

The old house is one of Charleston's most delightful single houses on one of the city's prettiest thoroughfares. For nearly two centuries it has been in the hands of owners who have kept it well and changed it little.

15 Legare — Light and airy house has changed little in two centuries.

Duelists Fired From Windows

A "celibate" husband, a third-story window duelist and "acorn" post ornaments that turned out to be pine cones or "pineapples" — all these are part of the history of the house at 14 Legare St.

While known as the Edwards House, it probably was built in 1801-1802 by Francis Simmons, a man who maintained his wife in a separate dwelling on Tradd Street from the day of their wedding. Simmons bought the property in 1800 for about $5,400.

The first house on the lot was recorded in 1779 and a brick building was there in 1784 — but Simmons no doubt erected the major part of the three-story mansion. He sold the property in 1816 to George Edwards for $20,000.

Edwards was to enlarge and elaborate the premises by purchase of the lot to the south in 1818. He moved a house on this lot to No. 1 Legare St. where it still stands. He then created a garden from the extra lot.

Francis Simmons married Miss Ruth Lowndes. After the wedding he escorted her to a handsome house on Tradd Street. Tradition has it that he went back to 14 Legare where he remained in residence for years. He called regularly at the Tradd Street house and presided at dinner parties and receptions there, always leaving just after the final guest departed.

According to legend, when the husband and wife rode in their separate carriages around The Battery and happened to meet, each would rise from the carriage seat. He would bow, she would curtsy, and go on their separate ways. The cause of this unusual marriage arrangement was never disclosed to the public, although members of the family are supposed to have known.

A fatal duel is reported to have been fought between No. 14 Legare and No. 15, just across the way. One dueler was in the

Detail of "pineapple."

southwest third story bedroom of No. 14. The other was in the northeast third story bedroom of No. 15. The one in No. 14 was killed and bloodstains remained on the bedroom floor for many years, a sure-fire item for scaring youngsters.

The handsome ironwork was installed by George Edwards, a wealthy merchant-planter whose family owned Spring Island near Beaufort. His initials are in the ironwork on either side of the stately door that opens above the white marble steps. Granite posts along the curbing were placed there to prevent carriages from being driven upon the sidewalk.

Edwards sold the house in 1835. The lot, which shows on the map of 1685, was part of an original grant to Richard Phillips. Ralph Izard, of the wealthy Goose Creek family, bought it in 1694 and it was sold by that family to Bernard Elliott in 1767, twelve years before a house was erected on it. The lot fronts 104 feet on Legare Street and extends 279 feet into the center of the block.

The house was owned by J. Adger Smyth from 1880 until 1930, and he lived in it while he was mayor of Charleston. It was acquired in 1930 by Walter J. Salmon, a New Yorker who used it as a winter residence. Mr. and Mrs. Victor J. Morawetz

bought it from Salmon and lavished money and care on its restoration.

The Edwards ironwork shows the Regency style that followed the French Empire era, fairly well dating this work as after 1816. The house itself is of the Adam architectural style.

Edwards ordered from Italy a set of live-oak acorns in marble. The Italian stonemasons turned out beautifully carved "pine cones," a distinctive form of pilaster decoration popular in the Mediterranean countries. It can be surmised that Edwards sent sketches to Italy and the workmen there simply assumed the sketcher didn't really know what he wanted.

While the "pine cone" finials resemble pineapples, they were copies originally of the cone of the Italian stone pine (*Pinus Pinea*) and were widely used during the Classical period in Italy. The pineapple was introduced to the Mediterranean area by the Portuguese about 1500 but was not widely known there until much later. However, the similarity in shape of the pineapple and the stone pine cone led to a confusion of the two names.

The gates of No. 14 Legare St. have been known for so long as the "Pineapple Gates" that the name probably will stick.

14 Legare — Unusual gatepost finials were carved by Italian craftsmen.

Scientist Watched Whale Hunt From Veranda Of His Home

The Charleston Museum's whale skeleton was preserved by the scientist-owner of 6 Gibbes St. who was able, in 1880, to see the harbor from the wide veranda of the handsome residence.

From that vantage point, Charleston Harbor's one-and-only whaling expedition was visible. Nearly 100 boats took part in the quite unhospitable treatment given the whale after it blundered into the harbor and couldn't find its way back to sea.

The fact that Dr. Gabriel Edward Manigault, an osteologist and educator of note, was able to flense the carcass and preserve it as a museum piece is in keeping with the abilities of the house's owners through the years. All have been able people and community leaders, quite in keeping with the style and dignity of the house.

It was built about 1800 on what was then the westernmost lot north of Gibbes Street. Wide marshes and oyster reefs stretched along the Ashley River to where the Coast Guard Base now stands and southwesterly there opened a magnificent vista of the Ashley with the woodlands of James Island as a backdrop.

Isaac Parker bought the lot in 1800 from the Gibbes family who occupied the magnificent pre-Revolutionary Georgian mansion at 64 South Battery. Parker was a planter and brickyard owner residing in St. Thomas and St. Denis Parish where his plantation fronted on Cooper River opposite the present Charleston Naval Base.

The $1,600 he paid for the 100-foot frontage lot reflected the prosperity of the area at that time. The house he started is of cypress above a brick foundation, probably baked at Parker's own factory and barged downriver to the building site. The property was sold 16 years later to Mrs. Susanne Forrester for $10,000, the price indicating a substantial dwelling had been built on it since Parker's acquisition.

Mrs. Forrester added 25 feet to the lot and when her executors sold it to Col. William Drayton, it fetched $12,500. Col. Drayton's military title came out of the War of 1812 and he used it although he was a lawyer and a leading member of the South Carolina bar.

It was Drayton who used a cash prize he had won in one of the lotteries that were so popular then (churches were quite fond of raising money that way) to add another 25-foot-wide parcel to the original lot and to extend the house at either end.

In 1837 he sold it to his wife's uncle, Nathaniel Heyward, one of the wealthiest rice planters of all time. Heyward owned 17 plantation and liked playing the role of the generous relative. He gave nine houses to kinspeople, 6 Gibbes being bestowed on his daughter, Elizabeth. Her husband, Charles Manigault, also was of a family of great wealth. His great-grandfather, whose ancestors had fled Huguenot persecution in Roman Catholic France with hardly a sou, had become so prosperous that he lent the fledgling State of South Carolina $220,000 and wrote off 80 per cent of the loan when the state finally got around to trying to repay him.

Charles Manigault and his son, Gabriel Edward Manigault who later inherited the property, were educated abroad and widely traveled. By combining Heyward and Manigault tastes and heirlooms, they created at 6 Gibbes St. a museum of fine art. Paintings by Le Bru and Copley shared honors with the very long fingernails of an ancient Chinese aristocrat.

Dr. Gabriel Edward Manigault, whose whale-preservationist activity is well remembered, left more than a rack of cetaceous bones to Charleston. He was a graduate of the College of Charleston and the S.C. Medical College (forerunner of the present Medical University of South Carolina) before he furthered his medical knowledge by attending schools in France. During the Civil War, he was an officer in the Confederate Army, returning to his native city to play a major role in the battle to restore some of its cultural and educational strength. As a professor at the College of Charleston, he took over management of the museum, then a part of the college where it had been established in 1814. Manigault acted as janitor, taxidermist, lecturer and curator for the museum, all without pay. He put his not small architectural talents to work in supervising restoration of the college's main buildings following the 1886 earthquake.

Manigault also revived the defunct Carolina Art Association and kept it going during his lifetime. As a hobby, he laid the handsome parquet floors in the two large parlors of 6 Gibbes St., a residence shared with his brother's family.

The house was sold by the Manigaults in 1899 to E.F. Mayberry who operated the University School, one of the first of Charleston's post Civil War private Schools. The house subsequently has had a number of owners.

6 Gibbes — House originally had a magnificent view of the Ashley River.

64 South Battery — House was built shortly after 1772.

Shipowner Built House To 'Receipt'

Builders of the pre-Revolutionary Georgian mansion at 64 South Battery complied explicitly with the Tidewater "receipt" prescribing that a house be placed "facing the water on the north or east side of the river so that the southwesterly summer sea breeze may be enjoyed."

When built, shortly after 1772, it was the most westerly house on South Bay (now South Battery) and it faced the Ashley river with James Island across the way.

William Gibbes, a wealthy shipowner and merchant, built the house immediately behind his "bridge" (wharf), which ran several hundred feet to the Ashley River channel.

Gibbes took part in the Revolution and returned with pleasure to his house and the "genteel entertainment" Charlestonians enjoyed on the end of his wharf during hot weather. After his death, Mrs. Sarah Moore Smith obtained the property and it remained in her family for the next four generations.

It was the residence of the family of John B.E. Sloan, a Charleston phosphate and cotton factor, during this century's first three decades.

In the 1930s the house was bought by Mrs. Washington A. Roebling, widow of the builder of the Brooklyn Bridge, and was somewhat altered and completely renovated. The main floor's southeast room was remodeled in Chinese Chippendale style to house her Oriental collections. The rear rooms were lengthened and brick stairs were placed to the rear leading to the formal gardens.

The original Georgian house had undergone some change in 1800 when Mrs. Smith installed fashionable Adam decorations throughout. She also added the grand marble front stairways, placed a high cove in the drawing room ceiling, installed wider mantel shelves and dressed up the handsome, but simple, Georgian woodwork with hard putty ornaments.

Mrs. Smith's grandson, Thomas Smith

Grimke, was one of Charleston's most brilliant lawyers. His son, the Rev. John Grimke Drayton (he took his mother's surname to inherit Magnolia Plantation) was the founder of Magnolia Gardens after "clergyman's throat" forced him to abandon an active ministry in the Episcopal Church.

While 64 South Battery possessed a garden during its early years, the present formal gardens were not created until Mrs. Roebling acquired the property.

The house still looks southward to the river, but population increases have placed houses between it and the water. The building of Murray Boulevard, and subsequent creation of "high land" behind it, blocked the Ashley's waters from their twice daily sweep to the great house's front yard.

Still, the house sits serenely before its handsome gardens, effectively giving them privacy, a grand example of the Georgian mansion in Charleston's "double house" style.

House Built On Log Cribbing Has Anti-Earthquake Feature

Whether by chance or design, the 1827 house at 39 South Battery incorporates an anti-earthquake feature that Frank Lloyd Wright used successfully for many years.

This charming antebellum house is built on a crib of palmetto logs sunk in mud, a fact that allowed it to sway with the tremors that literally wrecked most of Charleston in 1886. It was one of the few houses to survive the earthquake almost intact and, to this day, the owners say it sways slightly in gale or hurricane winds.

But it doesn't crack. Wright's architectural genius found itself the object of disbelief when he announced he would build Tokyo's Imperial Hotel on a floating foundation and predicted it would survive the earthquakes that plague Japan.

The hotel lived up to his predictions and stood undamaged in the Sept. 1, 1923, quake that knocked down 54 per cent of Tokyo's brick buildings and killed more than 100,000 persons in Japan.

The house at 39 South Battery was built atop a crisscrossed foundation of palmetto logs that rests on sand and pluff mud. There are two tales concerning the origin of the foundation. The house was constructed by the Magwood family and some descendants believe the builder deliberately constructed the supporting mudsill arrangement.

The other story is that the site was a spot on which a fort had been built much earlier. This redoubt reportedly was fashioned along the lines of the palmetto log fort on Sullivan's Island that became known as Fort Moultrie after it successfully stood off a British fleet in 1776.

While most of the fortifications of the original city were farther eastward and mainly along the Cooper River front, there is evidence that some fortified spots existed along the Ashley marshes. This could have been one of them.

At any rate, the house sits securely atop a foundation that allows sway to prevent breakage when earthquakes occur. It was known as the Moreland house for many years, a daughter of its builder having married a Moreland and inherited the dwelling.

When built, it was the only substantial house on the south side of South Battery west of King Street. South Battery's name was then South Bay and had been Fort Street when its first section was opened as far west as King Street.

The house very narrowly escaped being torn down on two occasions. During the 1850s, Mayor W.P., Miles announced a plan to create a large park at White Point Garden, then only about a third of its present size. The city purchased the Magwood-Moreland house and planned to fill the adjoining marshes and create a 15-acre park along the waterfront to the west.

The Civil War intervened and the house was ordered razed as a defense measure but the order was never carried out. Subsequently the city sold the house back into private ownership where it has remained ever since.

The proposed development of a public garden along the waterfront was made shortly after 1830 when the city purchased part of White Point. The city extended King Street almost down to what is now Murray Boulevard, erecting a tabby-work breakwater along its side.

This left a beach area between King Street and the 39 South Battery property to the west. It was used as a boat landing for many years and some residents of the area opposed construction of the Fort Sumter Hotel (now a condominium) there on the grounds that the property was dedicated to public usage. They failed, however, and Murray Boulevard was extended westward with the marshes behind it being filled to create building lots.

This effectively sealed off the Magwood-Moreland house from the waterfront it once owned, but its long porches still catch the sea breezes. When built, the house had only the lower piazza, the upper apparently having been added later.

It is a typical Charleston single house with a central stair hall flanked by sizeable rooms and a narrower wing extending southward. The house has beautiful woodwork and its carefully planned dimensions accomplish a most pleasing effect.

In one of its major rooms is an iron and brass fireplace apron that somehow had been removed from the house at one time. It was discovered in a nearby residence by one of the owners and retrieved to be returned to the fireplace for which it had been custom tailored.

The house has survived wars, rumors of wars, hurricanes and the hand of man. Should Charleston be so unfortunate as to undergo another major earthquake, 39 South Battery, thanks to its foundation, probably will sway, but remain standing.

39 South Battery — Unusual foundation provides safety.

Dwelling Cost Man His Bride

It's known as "O'Donnell's Folly" but it's one of Charleston's handsomest dwellings.

The house at 21 King St. also may have been the birthplace of the South Carolina Poetry Society and in it at one time lived the woman who was the inspiration for "Melanie" in Margaret Mitchel's "Gone With the Wind."

For about 25 years in the 1960-1980 period, this house was the site of the annual "Winter Games and Rout" of the Piping and Marching Society of Lower Chalmers Street, a Charleston philosophical society.

The kitchen wing of the house dates between 1725 and 1750. The library section, built about 1800, was restored in 1887 after the 1886 earthquake. The main house was built between 1852 and 1856.

It is the main house that catches the eye, its late Italian Renaissance styling soaring skyward and its well-balanced proportions offsetting rather heavy decorations on the facade.

A close examination of the house discloses many "extras" built into it by the Irish immigrant, Patrick O'Donnell. The huge timbers, thick brickwork and other structural details are much stronger than usually found in buildings of its day. That may be why it survived the earthquake when the 1800 library collapsed.

At any rate, O'Donnell set out to build a house for his bride-to-be, a house that would stand out in an area of outstanding houses.

And so he did, but at the cost of his love.

For — so the legend has it — the house was so long in the building that O'Donnell's fiancee married someone else, leaving the Galway Irishman with a tall house and many bedrooms, but no wife to help fill them.

O'Donnell lived there until his death in 1882 and died a bachelor. He left all his estate to be adminstered by a priest named "Father Tom Burke of the Order of St. Dominick" and to be used for the good of the poor of his native Galway.

Even in that most charitable effort, O'Donnell was doomed to defeat. The executor of his estate made off with most of the money. Father Burke died in 1883 and when the Bishop of Galway sued the executor there was no money left.

Sale of O'Donnell's real estate finally netted about $12,000 for the starving Irish.

At his death he had owned six other houses, all within a shillelagh toss of 21 King.

The house was bought by a fellow Gael, Thomas Riley McGahan, an unsuccessful member of the great California Gold Rush of 1849. McGahan had arrived in Charleston in 1853 and was in the dry goods businss when the Civil War began. He spent the war on various blockade runners. He was on the *Cecile* when she sank and on the Confederate Cruiser *Fox* when she made a daring daylight run through the Federal blockade off Galveston.

His wife was Emma Fourgeaud whose ancestors escaped from the massacre by slaves in Santo Domingo. Margaret Mitchell was a cousin of McGahan and was so impressed with the romantic tales of the flight of the Fourgeauds that she patterned "Melanie" after McGahan's wife.

Thomas Pinckney bought No. 21 in 1907. His daughter, Josephine, was then 12 years old. She grew up in the house and it was here, or at a Gibbes Street residence, during the so-called "Charleston Renaissance" era that the Poetry Society of South Carolina was formed.

Mr. and Mrs. Frederick Rutledge Baker obtained the house in 1937. It was purchased in 1962 by Mr. and Mrs. L. Louis Green III who completely restored the dwelling.

The lot is one of the oldest land delineations in the state, being granted to John Stevens in 1695. It was bought in 1722 from William Wallace by Thomas Lamboll. For many years the Lambolls lived in the house immediately south, No. 19 King. The City of Charleston subsequently bought No. 19 and sold it to O'Donnell who, as part of the purchase contract, moved it northward about 18 feet to permit Lamboll Street to be straightened.

The dwelling probably was designed by Edward C. Jones, a Charleston architect, whose work it strongly resembles.

The architect achieved the effect of an 18th century Venetian palazzo exterior wrapped around a cross-ventilated New York Brownstone townhouse interior set behind a typical Charleston array of wide piazzas.

The piazzas balance an unusually large entrance hall which provides a magnificent stairway along the northern wall.

The entry door is a massive one, standing above a flight of brownstone steps that were made unusually steep to be in correct scale with the building. An Italian "false perspective" architectural stratagem was used to make these appear larger than they are. The foot of the stairs is splayed well beyond the normal length, pushing the bottom stone abutments beyond the center line of the pilasters. These panelled pilasters and heavy classical entablature form a handsome door surrounding.

The second-floor window surrounds contain carved shells and other sea motifs.

The cast iron gas lamps are antiques and the two hitching posts were cast from old patterns of the 1800 era.

21 King — O'Donnell's Folly is a handsome dwelling.

Residence Attracted Invaders

The house at 27 King St. was described by an architectural historian as "the supreme example of the Charleston double house and perhaps the finest of American town houses."

Its "High Georgian" style and top quality workmanship qualify the Miles Brewton House as one of the finest jobs of architecture of the late 18th century to be found in the 13 original colonies.

That it was Charleston's finest residence is attested by the fact that commanding officers of two invading armies selected it as headquarters. British military leaders, Sir Henry Clinton and Lords Rawdon and Cornwallis, lived there during the occupation of the city in the Revolutionary War. Union Gens. Hatch and Meade, stayed in it after the surrender of Charleston.

Several years ago it was designated a National Historic Landmark by the Department of Interior. This recognition is limited to sites possessing exceptional value as commemorating or illustrating United States history.

The house was completed in 1769 for Miles Brewton, wealthy Charleston businessman and leader. Its builder was Ezra White, who came to Charleston from England and advertised himself as "Civil Architect, House Builder in general and Carver from London."

The square, brick building is in the pure Georgian style and was built during an era when the simple balance of this type of architecture was at its best. Distinction was added by placing of the two-tier portico on the face. The portico has pillars of Portland stone painted white. All wood and stone features on the portico are richly carved justifying the builder's description of himself as a "carver."

One of America's most outstanding rooms is the large drawing room on the second floor. It has escaped change and still has its original Waterford crystal chandelier. One reason for the excellent condition of the house and its escape from war damage was the fact that it was occupied by the highest ranking military invaders. Their presence prevented looting or vandalism by troops who treated other houses less decently.

The fully paneled rooms with carved enrichments and marble mantels all attest the good taste of Brewton and the capability of his builder. Its lower floor is paved with imported flagstone.

During the time it was occupied by the British, its owner, Rebecca Motte, remained in the house and presided at meals, treating her unwelcomed military guests with cold disdain. She had hidden her pretty daughters in the attic, believing the British did not know they were there.

27 King — Headquarters of British, Union commanders.

However, the story goes, that the British commander, bidding Mrs. Motte farewell, rolled his eyes significantly toward the ceiling and expressed regret at not having been able to meet the rest of her family.

One of the British officers carved a profile of the head of his commanding officer, Sir Henry Clinton, on one of the marble mantels and also the outline of a full-rigged ship, probably using a knife or the point of a bayonet as a tool. The "portrait" and the drawing of the ship are still clearly visible, long-lasting reminders of the role played by the house in America's bid for freedom from Great Britain.

The house has been owned through the years by descendants of the original family. In recent years it was the property of the Misses Frost and later the residence of Mr. and Mrs. Edward Manigault.

The houses has unusually large grounds and a picturesque group of outbuildings along the northern side of its lot. Wrought iron fencing opens up the front of the house to the street, giving an air of invitation. Very tall brick walls on either side efford privacy to the gardens behind them.

Etching of Ship.   **Profile of Gen. Clinton.**

Pirate Loot Is Rumored Buried Here

A two-fisted general and a courtly ladies man, Pierre Gustave Toutant Beauregard, once lived in 37 Meeting St.

But that's not why Old Charleston refers to it as the "Double-Breasted" house, or the "Bosoms." Its twin bays, curving symmetrically from each side of its massive entrance door, gave it that bosomy sobriquet long before the Civil War brought Gen. Beauregard here from New Orleans.

It also has a pirate legend, usually not believed by its owners but a great influence on children and servants. While it has no ghosts of record, its neighbor to the north was literally full of specters, according to an Episcopalian priest who lived there years ago.

Very little is known of Beauregard's short stay in the house except that he probably had ulcers. At any rate, he had stomach trouble and, because of the ailment, kept his own personal cow in the back yard while stationed in Charleston.

Regardless of its importance as the 1861 headquarters for "Old Bory," the house is an important architectural departure from the Charleston "norm." It sits square to the street, eschewing the Charleston practice of placing houses end-on or of squatting them right on the sidewalk line.

It also dates from before the Revolution, a fact that made it a witness to major events in this nation's major wars prior to the 20th century. Its unusual facade design hints at the use of an architect of some sort, although they were not known by that title in colonial America.

The old house has very large rooms and its first floor ceilings are higher than most. It is of stucco over a solid brick wall nearly two feet thick. The two large bay windows give the main rooms more light than is customary in houses of the period and also soften both the interior and exterior austerity of the house.

Its builder was probably James Simmons who died in 1775 and in his will mentioned the lot as "THE PLACE WHERE I now live." Traditions give the date of its construction as 1760. Gov. Robert Gibbes was the next owner and he also mentioned the house in his will, probated in 1782.

The Gibbes family had the house taken from them during the British occupation of the city in the Revolutionary War. When they got it back, it had been ransacked and vandalized. A family Bible was one of the few items saved, and it was half burned.

The house was built on the south portion of Lot 278 of the Grand Modell of Charles Towne, an area that was a sort of knoll with the marshes and waters of Vanderhorst's Creek making it a sort of peninsula at high tide. And that's all it took to get a pirate treasure-trove legend started, one

37 Meeting — Twin bays curve symmetrically from each side of entrance.

that probably had very little, if any, basis in fact.

At any rate, a pirate crew was supposed to have buried some loot on the knoll. Returning to their ship, the chief buccaneer found one man was missing. He hurried back to the knoll, surprised the wayward pirate digging up the gold, shot him and left him there with the loot.

According to Miss Caroline Conner, her brother, Henry W. Conner, used to dig in the back yard when he was a child. He never found any treasure, but the children, and the Conner servants, sincerely believed in the pirate ghost and didn't wander outside after dark.

When Gen. Beauregard arrived in Charleston March 1, 1861, he already was something of a legend. As a young lieutenant, his advice regarding the storming of Mexico City gave the Halls of Monetezuma to the American forces. Beauregard had just been named superintendent of the U.S. Military Academy at West Point when the Confederacy seceded from the Union. His resignation from the U.S. Army had not been acted on in Washington when President Jefferson Davis made him a brigadier general.

Confederate Army Headquarters had been set up in the now demolished Charleston Hotel and "Old Bory" lived there for a

time before setting up his offices in the house that was to be known as the "Executive Headquarters House." The Charleston Daily Courier commented on March 3, 1861, "The office of Gen. Beauregard, commanding the Confederate forces and volunteers here, is in the Executive Headquarters House on Meeting Street."

When Federal guns began long-range bombardment of Charleston Aug. 22, 1863, Beauregard charged U.S. Army Gen. Quincy A. Gillmore with "inexcusable barbarity" in his cannon assaults on "the old men, the women and children and the hospitals of a sleeping city."

The shelling forced removal of the CSA headquarters from downtown Charleston, and Beauregard's last offices in the city were on Ashley Avenue between Doughty and Bee Streets, beyond range of the Union guns.

After the Gibbes dynasty, the house was owned by William Brisbane and Otis Mills. Each of these owners changed it somewhat and Gen. James Conner completed its retoration following the Civil War.

During the 1950s the house was owned by Frank B. Gilbreth, former assistant publisher of the Charleston newspapers and author of a number of books, including "Cheaper by the Dozen."

34 Meeting — Built about 1760, this house was the residence of South Carolina's last royal governor and is considered one of the outstanding houses in the city.

Patriot Tricked Royal Governor

The house at 34 Meeting St. overlooks its garden behind balustraded walls, a serenely handsome facade of weathered stucco giving no hint of the exciting indidents that have occurred there.

It was a young house when the American Revolution began, having been built about 1760 by one or more of three persons: Capt. John Bull, Mrs. John Bull, or Mrs. Mary Blake. Its solid walls utilized the oversized clay-and-sand brick of Low-country riverside brickyards, a brick that weathers to a beautiful and distinctive patina but which has little structural strength, necessitating very thick walls whenever multi-storied buildings were constructed.

It is of the usual Charleston double-house pattern. The handsome entrance hall runs across the width of the house at its longitudinal center and there are two rooms on each side. Double-flight stairs, with solid mahogany rails, are on each of the three floors that rise above the cellar.

The interior wood and plaster work reflects an era when the former frontier colony was producing individuals prosperous enough to afford expensive ornamentation in residences. The house has a particularly beautiful second-floor drawing room ceiling. The paneling throughout is handsome and that of the drawing room was designed as a background for long mirrors. These hung on the walls until Union Army occupation troops arrived in Charleston during the waning days of the

Civil War. The mirrors and most of the house's valuable furniture were stolen and shipped north.

Three piazzas look over the garden, catching the cooling sea breeze in summer and trapping warmth from the low-riding sun in winter. The piazzas were added after 1900.

When built the house sat on the front of a lot that sloped gradually to the east. A small creek meandered through salt marshes there and emptied into Charleston Harbor where Water Street now meets East Bay. Houses now stand in the former "back yard" of 34 Meeting, and the creek long since has been filled and made into high land.

The marsh creek, the high-ceiled drawing room and the stucco pediment cornice all figured in events that took place in the house. It was in the drawing room on Sept. 13, 1775, that Capt. Adam McDonald of the First Regiment of Provincial Infantry played a role that helped solidify South Carolinians in opposition to the British Crown. Posing as a sergeant in an Upcountry Tory troop, McDonald tricked South Carolina's last royal governor, Lord William Campbell, into disclosing King George's plans to send troops to destroy the colonial forces. The next night, realizing he had been outwitted, Campbell boarded a small boat in the marshes and escaped to a British man-of-war anchored in Rebellion Roads, down the harbor.

He returned nine months later with Sir Peter Parker's fleet and took part in the unsuccessful attack on Charleston in which a tiny palmetto log fort on Sullivan's Island defeated the British. Campbell died later of wounds received in the battle. His flight had resulted in dispersal of the Tory forces in the Piedmont and placed the Revolutionists in complete charge of the state.

The house became a property of the Huger family following the Revolution. Francis Kinloch Huger, a boy at the time, was standing on the front steps shortly after the Revolution when a piece of mortar fell from the roof, striking him on the head. He lived to be the hero of the abortive attempt to rescue Lafayette from Austria's Olmutz Prison in 1794. When Lafayette visited Charleston in 1825, he was entertained here by the Hugers. In 1886, when the great earthquake shook Charleston, the mortar, that had replaced the fallen piece, fell. This time it struck a visiting Englishman and killed him.

The residence, one of Charleston's oldest and most outstanding dwelling houses, has remained in possession of the Huger family.

During its more than 200 years, some liberties have been taken with the original building but, basically, it is the same house that was built for a well-to-do 18th century family in the street that ran alongside the old walled city of Charles Towne a block to the north.

Chimneys Hid Hessian Troops Deserting After Revolution

Some of Charleston's oldest German families are descended from Hessian troops who were quartered in the house at 30 Meeting St. during the Revolutionary War.

The Hessians, King George's mercenaries, deserted in large numbers when the war was over. When orders were issued for the troops to board the British warships and leave Charleston, many of the Hessians fled to the hinterlands.

Legend has it that some of the officers and men hid in the broad chimneys of 30 Meeting St. until the Redcoat roundup was over. It is known that Charleston experienced an unexplained increase in citizens with Germanic sounding names immediately after hostilities ceased.

If the German troops did, indeed, take "French leave" in this house, it is a paradox for the dwelling was the home of Isaac Motte and a more revolutionary clan of French Huguenots is not known to have existed.

Col. Motte also owned Exeter Plantation on the upper Cooper River. That holding was a part of the original Fairlawn Barony. Its beautiful pre-Revolutionary house burned in 1967.

Motte apparently completed this house after it had been started by Thomas Young. The Mottes bought it from Young in 1770, and the house was destined to remain in the hands of their descendants for 147 years. It has been called the Motte House and the Haig House by various generations of Charlestonians.

The house was bought in 1947 by Mrs. Victor Morawetz from the estates of Motte Haig and Charles Haig. Mrs. Morawetz refurbished it and turned its servants' house and kitchen into a separate one-family dwelling. She had the beautiful cypress paneling restored to its natural state and removed a layer of stucco from the solid brick walls along the porches.

The house is typical of the earlier Georgian style of architecture as adapted to Charleston before the Revolution. Its massive moldings and wide paneling reflect this type of decor at its peak.

No. 30 Meeting has a fairly large lot measuring 80 feet on the street and extending 237 feet into the center of the block.

It is flanked by similarly large mansions built in different styles. In 1770 this part of downtown Charleston had become the most fashionable part of the prosperous colonial seat and Isaac Motte no doubt saw to it that his town house was of the best materials.

Three broad piazzas flare out across the entire length of the house, affording shade in summer and a sunny "cooter bank" in winter. The high garden wall is typical of the screens built to assure privacy. The entry door, set in the street end of the lower porch, is the hallmark of Charleston's single houses.

The house displays the artisanship and meticulous care of its builders. Its staircase has a shadow rail and dado all the way to the attic. The first-floor drawing room has fielded paneling and a beautifully executed chimneypiece. The paneling in the dining room is of the flat Georgian type, however. The full paneling is continued in the main rooms of the second story, including the master bedroom.

30 Meeting — Georgian single house was refurbished in 1947.

1792 Building Reflects Many Changes

No. 31 Meeting St. was one of the first Charleston dwellings to install gaslights in the antebellum era and one of the first of the old houses to be wired for electricity in later years.

It also is a reflection of many changes wrought in the building by its various owners. The delightfully Victorian Gothic "tea house" in its garden is only one symbol of the architectural styles imposed on the original structure.

The dwelling was built in 1792 by Lt. Gov. James Ladson, a member of a wealthy family of plantation owners. In those days the house opened on Ladson's Court (now Ladson Street) to the north. It was a typical Charleston "single house" with its north door leading into a hall that traverses the building. The present front entrance opens onto a piazza on the garden side. The change was made in the 1840s.

Despite the many changes, some of the original woodwork still remains on the first two floors. After Ladson's widow died, the property was acquired by Jeremiah A. Yates whose brother, Joseph, owned 27 Meeting St. One of the second floor mantels is similar to those in 27 Meeting.

In 1832 Charles M. Furman, a banker, bought the house. He sold it in 1844 to Erastus M. Beach who drastically changed it. Beach added the piazzas on the garden side and squared off the third floor, adding the Empire era parapet roof line that exists today. Beach also erected the wrought iron fence and installed classic revival doors on both the Ladson Street and porch entrances.

The entrance hall was rearranged by Beach, the stairway being changed to coincide with the new front door location. Beach installed three black marble mantels, typical of ones in the 1840-50 period.

The house was one of the first in Charleston to be piped for gaslights and two lovely crystal chandeliers, installed by Beach, still remain.

The Victorian aspects of the present house date from after 1877 when Christopher P. Poppenheim bought the place following the death of Beach's window. Poppenheim was a disabled Confederate veteran who owned a Cooper River rice plantation and conducted a hardware business on King Street.

He built the large, two-story bay fronting on Meeting Street and added a dining room. The charming tea house was part of a garden that included an olive tree, 20 orange trees, kumquats and other tropical shrubs, all planted by him.

Japanese laborers, brought to Cooper River after the Civil War to work the Poppenheim rice crops, laid the herringbone design brick in the garden walks. The wrought iron pedestrian gate on Meeting

31 Meeting — House shows Empire, Victorian and Georgian influences.

Street was installed by Poppenheim.

The 1886 earthquake undid some of Poppenheim's remodeling and the characteristic "X" shaped cracks that earth tremors leave in masonry showed up in the plaster walls of many of the rooms. The Charleston tornado of 1938 seriously damaged the building, leaving the north weatherboarding detached from the house.

Poppenheim had four daughters, all of whom graduated from Vassar College, the first women from Charleston to attend that northern institution. One, Miss Mary B. Poppenheim, was a charter member and (in 1917-19) president general of the United Daughters of the Confederacy. She was responsible for the founding of the Paris, France, branch of the UDC.

With her sister, Louisa, she was an activist for equal rights for women. She participated in suffragist campaigns and took part in a 30-year struggle that finally saw coeds admitted to the College of Charleston in 1918.

The Poppenheim sisters, according to a contemporary, were "wedded to the past," and their home was almost a museum with its Victorian furniture and other antiques.

Miss Louisa Poppenheim resisted change in practically everything except women's rights. When Tradd Street was changed from one-way west to one-way east, she continued to drive westward on that thoroughfare, much to the consternation of other motorists and the dismay of police who were cowed by her gentle, but terribly firm, admonishments.

The Poppenheims installed the fountain in the garden with the delightful figure of Narcissus, said to be a duplicate of one in the Kaiserhof Gardens at Bad Neuheim, Germany.

Mr. and Mrs. Craig M. Bennett, who bought the property about 1959, renovated the interior of the dwelling and restored a pre-existing Georgian-designed garden in front of the house. They also hung a pair of beautiful wrought iron gates at the vehicle entrance on Ladson Street. The gates date from the early 19th century and formerly were on Charlotte Street. They were redesigned for the new location and a large brass sunburst center was added.

The tropical trees of the Poppenheim garden were killed by cold weather some years ago but the garden still contains many old camellias and other Charleston garden favorites. It has a number of crepe myrtle trees, sego palms, actually a type of fern, and various relics of the past including pomegranate, tea olive and Chinese camphor trees.

Similarities And Differences Mark Trio Of Charleston Residences

Perhaps nowhere in Charleston is the similarity — and the differences — in its "single houses" so evident as in this trio of old dwellings on lower Meeting Street.

Each has its end to the street, but the ends differ in shape, width, height, architectural decor and color.

Each is a three-story building but two have garrets and one has a basement.

Each has a second-story balcony over the sidewalk. The wrought iron-supported platforms are of different size and shape, alike in that they open onto spacious drawing rooms but different because of small details.

Each has its wrought iron gate that affords the passerby a peek into shaded patio gardens that widen spaciously where the narrow outbuildings and rear flankers begin.

One of the houses — No. 23 — has Victorian "eyebrows" hooding its deep-set upper windows. It and its neighbor, No. 25, maintain the traditional Charleston habit of blinds on the first floor windows and louvered shutters above that level, a practice designed to prevent peeping by passersby. No. 27, however, has a low basement that lifts its first floor windows well above eye level of all but big league basketball stars and rendering blinds unnecessary.

No. 25 is thought to be the oldest of the trio, dating to about 1760. The post-Revolutionary house at 27 Meeting has an unusually lovely wrought iron gate of recent vintage but designed to fit perfectly into the old Charleston scene. Date of construction of No. 23 is not certain but probably before 1788.

In the early days of the port city, this section of Meeting Street was called "Meeting Street, Extended." At first it was separated from the main street which began just above the present site of Water Street where the old walled city had its southwestern corner. At that point a small marsh creek ran westward. It was an extension of Vanderhorst's Creek, the estuary that fronted the city's south wall. The marsh is now Price's Alley. Meeting Street consists of several layers of materials reflecting the roadway construction of different periods.

In descending order, one finds asphalt, brick, oyster shell, wood and a mixture of sand and shell. Also covered in modern years were two sets of trolley tracks, one wood and the other iron. The latter often plagues unwary waterworks crews when they try to lay new water mains.

The houses form one of the more picturesque groupings in Charleston. Viewed on a spring morning with sunlight funnelling down between the trees, their soft colors, charming facades and trim appearance do much to delight the eye.

An even prettier view is on a cold winter's night with a high-riding moon pen-

23-25-27 Meeting — A picturesque, colorful grouping.

etrating the shadows, spraying lacy patterns of limb shadow on the pavement and blending the pastel-colored walls into a sort of midnight magic. In that light, the spacious rooms, soft-lighted and dim, from across the street have the appearance of artificiality.

But they are very real and the two northerly ones represent two of the more affluent eras of Charleston's past. No. 25 was built when the colony was enjoying a boom under the status of a Royal Colony, having recovered from the troubles that beset it until the Lords Proprietor were displaced in the 1720s.

Its roof has a belled eave, the tip-tilted effect being carried out in the facade parapet. This slight upturn was devised to

send rainfall cascading away from the sides of the building and is found usually only on fairly steep roofs.

The northernmost house has a hip roof that is almost invisible above its severely decorous front. Its elegantly spiralled balcony ironwork and decorative buttress combine to soften the austere front.

The "eyebrows" over the windows at No. 23 probably were put on much later, possibly following the 1886 earthquake. At that time, a great many houses suffered heavy damage and late Victorian decorations were substituted because the original items could not be replaced.

Each of the graceful trio of houses is a single-family dwelling now, serving the purposes for which they were constructed nearly two centuries ago.

18 Meeting — House was built in Adam style without regard to expense.

Declaration Of Independence Signer Lived In This Dwelling

Thomas Heyward, signer of the Declaration of Independence, lived in the handsome brick dwelling at 18 Meeting St.

He also is believed to have been the first person to parody the words of the British national hymn, "God Save the King." However, Heyward's version did not gain the popularity of "My Country 'Tis of Thee" by a later author.

He probably built the house shortly after 1803, the year he bought the lot from his brother, Nathaniel. Thomas Heyward had been living on lower Church Street at the time, having sold his home at 87 Church St. to the Grimke family. That house is now known as the Heyward-Washington House because Heyward's old friend and fellow revolutionary, George Washington, stayed there during his triumphal tour of the nation in 1793.

By 1806 Heyward was living at 18 Meeting and occupied it until his death in 1809.

His brother, Nathaniel, bought the house from Thomas' widow in 1815 for $20,000 — a considerable sum at that time — and presented it to his daughter, Ann, who was married to Gabriel Henry Manigault.

A secret, or hidden, room in 18 Meeting is located on the second floor and quite likely was a wine closet. A similar room was discovered in the Gabriel Manigault mansion at the southeast corner of George and Meeting Streets when that fine old building was being demolished a number of years ago. That room, moreover, still contained a goodly supply of spirits.

In architectural style, the house is an exquisite example of the Charleston single house done in the high Adam style and with no regard for expense.

Spacious hallways extend the depth of the building, permitting wide stairways to the upper floors. The mahogany stair rail circles gracefully to the attic, ascending from a lower hall that has carved woodwork and fine cornices.

Huge pine beams, handwrought iron nails, wooden pegs and dowels are evident in the attic, denoting the antiquity of the house and also the meticulous care the builders took to achieve solidarity.

The living room on the front at street level is handsomely paneled to chair-rail height. Its cornice includes rosette and egg-and-dart carvings.

The second-floor drawing room has had its original wood mantel replaced by an ornate one of marble with a deep cut rose and ivy motif. Its wide frieze and cornices have carvings of grape leaves, grapes and other classical designs. The picture moldings are gilded and the carved window cornices are coated with gold leaf. A crystal chandelier hangs from a fine oval medallion ceiling.

Thomas Heyward's use of the British national hymn tune as an American patriotic song occurred July 4, 1781, while he and about 60 other prominent Charlestonians were prisoners of the British at St. Augustine, Fla.

They had been captured when Charleston fell the year before. Determined to celebrate the anniversary of the signing of the Declaration of Independence, they gathered food and wine and obtained permission from their guards to hold a noonday feast.

According to the story, Heyward wrote the words:

"God Save the Thirteen States
Thirteen United States,
God Save Them All."

The words were sung over and over to the tune "God Save the King." It was not until 1831, however, that Samuel Francis Smith put together and printed the now-familiar words of "America," and today only legend credits Heyward and that gallant band of prisoners for singing their country's praises under the very ears of British guards.

Three months later their prayers were answered when Cornwallis surrendered at Yorktown. He had lived in the Miles Brewton House at 27 King St., a block away from 18 Meeting and some of his officers had occupied Heyward's house on Church Street during British occupation of the city.

Heyward returned to his home and wide family connections to continue service to his state and nation. That work began in the S.C. House of Commons in 1772 and continued when he was one of the committee of 11 to draft the constitution that made South Carolina an independent nation in 1776.

That document contained the basis upon which the United States Constitution was conceived.

The house reflects the taste of a South Carolina gentleman who designed it as a town house of elegance and comfort for use when not managing his extensive plantation holdings in St. Luke's Parish south of Charleston.

16 Meeting — Victorian residence was built in 1876-78 and has about 24,000 square feet of living space.

Elaborate Mansion Has 35 Rooms

The 35-room Italianate-style mansion at 16 Meeting St. was built in 1876-78 for George Walton Williams, a successsful Charleston banker and businessman.

It is considered to be one of the most important Victorian houses on the Eastern seaboard and is one of only a few residences constructed in Charleston during the first two decades after the Civil War.

The house was meticulously restored in 1976-77 by Gedney M. Howe III, a Charleston lawyer, and is operated as a house museum with several apartments apart from the main rooms.

The mansion has about 24,000 square feet of living space, 14-foot ceilings, ornate plaster and wood moldings, elaborate chandeliers, a broad stairwell with a 75-foot domed ceiling. The central hall is 14 feet wide and 50 feet long.

There is a cupola atop the roof that affords a magnificent view of the lower city and of the harbor and its environs. Williams, who came to Charleston from North Carolina in the 1840s and made a fortune in wholesale groceries and banking, spared no expense, spending more than $200,000 on construction.

When it was completed, New York, Atlanta and Charleston newspaper accounts indicate it was one of the most elaborate and expensive mansions in the United States. The lot on which it was built was 183 feet across on Meeting Street and extended eastward all the way to Church Street. The rear portion later was sold and contains a separate residence.

The lot originally was occupied by the Edward Fenwick House, one of Charleston's grandest 18th century mansions that was demolished prior to the Civil War to make room for a proposed residence which never was built. Williams bought the property during the Civil War for $40,000 in Confederate currency. In 1869 he sold the lot to Launcelot Grimball, but regained possession in 1873 when Grimball went bankrupt.

A year later George W. Williams & Co. celebrated its 31st anniversary and Williams also opened his first bank. His firm apparently was the first large mercantile company to re-open its doors in Charleston following the Civil War.

Williams hired W.P. Russell as his architect.

The structure was built of small red brick laid in running or "standard" bond, a construction pattern not found in Charleston's antebellum buildings. In a variation from usual architecture, Russell installed wide windows with four sashes under a single eliptical arch.

The house has three front bays, the central one including the main entry. This bay has a pediment above the classic entablature around the building. The entry portico has two tiers of Corinthian columns and is reached by a double flight of stairs. Cathedral-sized doors open into the foyer which is paved with colored tiles and paneled in walnut with symbols of the Trinity inlaid in satinwood. This pattern continues in the great hall.

The main rooms and great hall on the first floor have plaster moldings and hand-painted scenes. The dining room has fleur-de-lis and flower basket decorations painted by Thomas Wightman.

Scenes depicting the four seasons on the ceiling of the great hall had been covered by three coats of paint. The Howes prevailed on an artist friend, Ken Mayes, to paint four portraits in the corner squares. In these, Patricia Howe is spring, Dianne Smith is summer, Howe is winter and Mayes is fall.

The music room rises two stories from the second floor immediately above the dining room. It continues above the roof level and has a 45-foot high ceiling with a coved glass skylight.

The exterior corners have quoins of blue-green slate, varying from the usual quoins on Charleston houses which are mainly of brick.

After Williams died, the property went to his son-in-law, Patrick Calhoun, a grandson of John C. Calhoun, the Great Nullifier and vice president of the United States. It was operated as a fashionable pension and then, in 1934, was sold by R.S. Manigault and associates to Vera McClure Findlay of Washington, D.C., for $25,000.

After World war II it was purchased by Charles E. Rausch, Charleston businessman and owner of the former Argyle Hotel. The house later became the property of Hollis E. Ayers and his wife, Dorothy Rausch Ayers, from whom Howe obtained it in 1976.

At that time the house was in need of complete refurbishing, a task that Howe, some of his friends and a contractor accomplished with loving care.

Residence Built In 1788 Once Housed Men's Club

Entrance of 7 Meeting St.

The house at 7 Meeting St. has memories of a famous punch, one of the most drawn-out poker hands ever played in Charleston and the shortest-lived "Ladies Day" in a men's club.

It also is notable because of its unusual construction and its beautiful simplicity of design in the grand Charleston "double house" style. For behind its "black" cypress weatherboarding is a layer of brick, giving added substance to one of the most durable woods used in house construction.

The house was built about 1788 and at that time commanded from its garden a handsome view of the Ashley River across what was then called South Bay (now South Battery). Today it still has spacious gardens but no longer a look at the river.

It was during its occupancy by the Charleston Club (1881-1927) that the famous "Charleston Club Punch" is first mentioned in the club's minutes although the receipt apparently came from J. Clarence Cochran, a member of the club in 1852. According to Thomas della Torre, College of Charleston professor and historian for the club in 1938, Cochran's receipt was preserved by Col. Aiken Simmons.

It called for "one volume green tea, one volume California brandy, one-fourth volume Santa Cruz rum, lemon juice and sugar to taste, ice, lemon peel and, just before serving, one volume mineral water." A postscript says: "California brandy blends better than French brandy; Santa Cruz white rum has the better taste. If Santa Cruz cannot be had, use Jamaica rum. Barcardi rum will not do."

The punch — always mixed in large amounts — became a most popular event. E.H. Sparkman apparently possessed a special aptitude for its preparation for the minutes of 1915 show that the secretary was instructed to ask Mr. Sparkman to "mix the same, as usual."

Club history states that an annual "Ladies Day" event was voted in by the members in 1891 and was voted out a year later. History does not disclose the reason, but the club has been an all-male institution since.

The club paid $11,000 for the house and sold it in 1927 to Eleanor Sophia Maybank for $25,000 to take up quarters elsewhere. The club had been founded in 1852. It was disbanded in 1866 in the aftermath of the Civil War and was reconstituted in 1881. During the interim, most of its members affiliated with the Carolina Club.

What may have been the most drawn-out poker hand ever played in Charleston occurred at a game between members of the Charleston Club in the days of unlimited betting. One player lived across the harbor in Mount Pleasant, which had no telephones at that time and which could be reached only by ferry.

Shortly before midnight, when the last ferry left, the Mount Pleasant player was facing a lone opponent, known as the slowest caller in the club. The pot was large — several hundred dollars — and a large bet had been made.

The ferryboat commuter figeted as the slow caller studied his cards. Finally, noting that it was 11:45, the commuter gave his poker hand to a friend and asked him to play it for him, promising to call from the ferry dock.

The ferry was about to pull out when he telephoned. The man still had not made up his mind to call the bet.

It was not until the next morning, when his friend met him at the ferry landing, that the commuter learned — nine hours later — that he had won the pot after his opponent had finally called.

The house was built by Josiah Smith who owned a large portion of the area on the west side of Meeting Street. The lane, now called "Little" Lamboll Street, originally was Smith Lane.

In 1800 the house was sold to Wilson Glover by Smith. It then was owned by John Huger, a son-in-law of Glover, who sold it to Miss Martha Prioleau.

Her estate sold it to Col. Thomas Y. Simons who added the wide piazzas on the south. The Charleston Club obtained it from the Simons family.

In 1937 the house was bought by Mr. and Mrs. H. Cecil Sharp of Islip, Long Island, who renovated it completely and raised the height of the wall to insure privacy in the gardens.

7 Meeting — Cypress weatherboarding covers layer of brick.

1 Meeting — Empire-period home has English-style basement.

Meeting Street Mansion Was Center Of Two Wars

The imposing mansion at 1 Meeting St. was in the center of two wars, one military, one legal. Both made history in Charleston.

The legal battle lasted 22 years, five times longer than the Civil War which also swirled around the house.

On its wide piazzas, friends and relatives of William Middleton, last of his surname to own the famous Middleton Place Gardens, gathered in the pre-dawn chill of April 12 to cheer the firing of a shell from Fort Johnson over Fort Sumter to herald the beginning of the Civil War.

The house survived that war without a scratch, a surprising feat considering its location in the lower part of the city which was heavily shelled by U.S. batteries on Morris Island.

The legal war ended with the house being converted into apartments and the subsequent sale of its outbuildings.

The late Empire period residence rises high above its English-style basement. The huge rooms and lofty ceilings prob-ably give it more cubic footage of space and fewer individual rooms than any of Charleston's other antebellum residences.

A Scotsman, John Robertson, had the house built in 1846. It is of solid construction, utilizing the out-sized "Charleston" brick made at brickyards along tidewater rivers, heart pine timbers and flooring and cypress from Lowcountry swamps. Its builder erected solid brick servants' quarters to the north. An annex that extended to the west end of the corner lot was torn down in 1961.

The massive iron lamps flanking the Meeting Street entrance to the house are unusual and quite ornate. These probably were placed by interim owners. Robertson sold the house shortly after it was built to William Middleton.

Middleton occupied it as a town house until 1870 when he sold it to Mrs. Alexander Ross. The house then entered a priod of fairly lonely occupancy for the Ross family consisted only of grown-ups. During the late 19th and early 20th centur-ies it was occupied by Miss Mary Jane Ross, the last of her family, who died in 1922 at the age of 90.

She had traveled extensively during her lifetime and the house was packed with mementoes from many lands. These included a hand-carved cabinet created from a mantel that once graced an Indian rajah's palace, a set of hand-crafted silver from Kashmir and Chinese and Japanese antiques.

Her will set up the house as a museum in memory of her brothers. Both of them fought with the Confederate Army, one being killed while serving with the Washington Light Infantry.

The reading of the will initiated one of the longest court cases ever to take place in this country. It began shortly after Miss Ross died and was not finally resolved until 1944. The litigation resulted in the museum trust being abolished. The Charleston Library Society, the First Presbyterian Church, the Medical Society of South Carolina (Roper Hospital) and Philadelphia Presbyterian Hospital received what was left of the estate. Legal fee claims of $92,438.03 where presented by a Charleston law firm and the widow of a Philadelphia lawyer who died during the litigation.

At that time (1944) this was the highest court fee ever awarded by a Charleston court. The claim was nullified on four occasions by the S.C. Supreme Court and subsequently settled for about $69,000. The estate amounted to more than $360,000.

Auction of the Ross collection of antiques and silver attracted one of the largest crowds ever to attend an auction here.

The house was bought from the Ross estate for $35,000 in 1945 by Mrs. Minnie S. Carr, owner of 2 Meeting St. just across the way. Mrs. Carr converted both the main house and its servants' quarters into apartments.

She later sold the house to Dr. and Mrs. John C. Hawk who changed it back into a single-family residence. A smaller unit at the rear of the South Battery vehicle entrance is rented. The former servants' building was sold separately and this smaller building, now No. 3 Meeting, has been remodelled into a charming residence.

During existence of the mansion as an apartment building, the basement was converted into a restaurant. It later became a temporary home for "Miss Mason's School," a private elementary day school. A seasonal tea shop was operated during the major tourist visitation period for several years.

The house has a hallway that is larger than many modern apartments. Its broad stairs sweep grandly upward and its main floor rooms are connected by massive sliding doors, enabling creation of a huge space for entertainment.

From its upper piazza, a magnificent view of the harbor is afforded and the orientation of the house, east-west athwart the path of Charleston's sea breeze, plus its airy rooms and large windows, make it an exceptionally comfortable residence in one of the city's most desirable locations.

8 South Battery — A fine example of the Charleston double house with two stories above the basement.

House Named For War Hero

The William Washington House at 8 South Battery was named for a cousin of George Washington whose military career in the Revolution rivaled that of his more famous kinsman.

And an impetuously romantic event gave him a bride and also a flag that today is still cherished by Charleston's Washington Light Infantry. It is the only Revolutionary War flag from active service still borne by a unit of the U.S. Army.

Col. William Washington of Stafford County, Va., was 20 years younger than his cousin, George, but he already was a war hero when he arrived in South Carolina in 1778 at the age of 26. Here he added laurels to his name and was a constant threat to the British until he received severe wounds at the Battle of Eutaw Springs.

He was captured and held prisoner in Charleston for the remainder of the war, the British refusing to exchange so capable a soldier who had given them so much trouble and who undoubtedly would have continued to do so had he been released.

The house he brought his bride to after the war had been built, probably in 1768, by Thomas Savage. Washington bought the house from Mrs. Mary Elliott Savage, widow of the builder and kinswoman of Washington's wife, Jane Elliott, who first captured the Virginian's fancy when she created the now famous "Eutaw Flag," carried by Col. Washington's troops as

their battle flag at both Cowpens and Eutaw Springs.

Washington's early military reputation was gained at the battles of Long Island (N.Y.), Trenton (N.J.) and Princeton (N.J.), and it is paradoxical that his major British foe, Banastre Tarleton, was somewhat responsible for gaining him both a flag and a bride.

Washington was sent to South Carolina as a lieutenant colonel when the British siege of Charleston was mounted. At Rantowles Bridge, 12 miles west of Charleston, on March 26, 1780, Washington, the Virginia cavalryman, and Tarleton, Sir Henry Clinton's girlish-faced but sadistic and brilliant fighter, met for the first time in battle.

Washington was leading the remnants of Bland's, Baylor's and Maylan's Virginia regiments of horse. Tarleton's Dragoons were moving north after landing near Savannah. The Americans drove the dragoons back, taking several prisoners including Col. John Hamilton, a N.C. Tory and experienced officer.

Sandy Hill plantation, owned by Charles Elliott, was scarcely a mile away and Col. Washington was relaxing there after the battle when he happened to mention that his cavalry unit did not have a flag. Miss Jane Elliott reportedly made a flag from a heavy, crimson, silk-fringed curtain. She placed it on a hickory pole and handed it

to Washington stating: "Here is your flag, Colonel." It led his cavalry when the Americans decisively routed the British at Cowpens and later at Eutaw when the British cut Washington's troops to pieces and captured him.

The flag was presented to the Washington Light Infantry April 19, 1827, by Washington's widow.

The Washingtons used 8 South Battery as a town house, living much of the year at Sandy Hill where Washington was buried.

The house is a fine example of the Charleston double house, with two stories above a brick basement. Its original entry apparently was on Church Street since early records list it as a Church Street house.

Today one enters onto wide piazzas on the western side from marble steps rising beside a formal garden.

There is a large drawing room and the major rooms are beautifully paneled. When the house was built, Church Street was a thoroughfare and South Bay, as it was then called, was a waterfront promenade extending only a short distance westward.

The house passed out of the Washington family prior to the Civil War. It was owned by Robert B. Dowie until 1915 when it was purchased by Julian Mitchell, Charleston banker and lawyer.

House Designed For Entertaining

One of Charleston's most imposing mansions was one of the last of the port city's "great houses" to be built.

The Villa Margherita, at 4 South Battery, stands on one of the original lots of the city. With its four-column portico, balconies, balustraded porch and shuttered windows, it is typical of the "Old Charleston" tradition, but the house was built about 1895.

Its builder, Andrew Simonds, was president of the First National Bank here and a leader in the economic development of the area. The architecture of the Villa is a variation on the "Chicago Exposition Style," combining several earlier period fashions.

Its site, overlooking White Point Garden and Charleston Harbor, is one of the most advantageous in the city, with the green foliage of the park affording a pleasing view and protection from storms.

The Villa was designed for entertaining on a lavish scale and was so used during the first decade of its existence. At that time the grounds at the rear, opening on Church Street, were laid out as a formal sunken garden. A great hall opens behind the massive front doors, extending to the patio between the rear wings, with a transeptal hall extending east and west.

Simonds died in 1905 and the Villa became a winter hostelry in 1909, a role it was to play until World War II began. Miss Ina Liese Dawson leased the building from Mrs. Simonds in 1914, named the house "Villa Margherita" and operated it in the manner of a fashionable European "pension." She added an annex at the rear of the lot.

Before Florida entered the picture and during the heyday of the "Yankee occupation" of South Carolina plantations as winter hunting preserves, the Villa became one of the better-known stopping places in the South.

Its guest list included Henry Ford, Alexander Graham Bell, Gen. Leonard Wood and other industry, government and society leaders. Service was perfect, cuisine superb, and the Villa's fame spread afield.

In 1942 the Villa was leased to United Seaman's Service and for three years was used by merchant seamen and their families. It reopened after the war as a hotel with little success.

Two fires and mortgage problems forced its closing in 1953. From 1954 until 1961 it was the private residence of Mr. and Mrs. Charles W. Waring, the latter being a daughter of the Simonds who built it.

In 1961 it was converted to a single-family residence. The rear additions were removed and the rear wings face a pool and patio, much the same as when the building went up near the turn of the century.

Prior to 1895 the lot was occupied by a typical Charleston single house with two long piazzas facing White Point Garden. The three-story-and-garret building was built prior to the Revolution and survived that war and the Civil War.

During the Civil War, White Point Garden was a military fortification with batteries and high-piled earthworks. The trees were very young then. Many survived leveling of the fortifications after the war and others were planted later.

Just to the southeast of the Villa Margherita site was the gallows from which pirates were hanged. There, at the edge of the marsh, Stede Bonnet and his crew swung in the breeze several days as a warning to others who might fancy the freebooter's life.

The Villa stands today behind its tall palms, a portrait of solid grandeur. To the older residents, the quasi-Greek revival features render it a bit out of place in old Charleston. But to the visitor, the Villa Margherita is typical of the old South and is one of the most photographed houses in the city.

4 South Battery — Residence spent many years as the Villa Margherita, a winter hostelry.

First Act Of 'Southern Tragedy' Seen From House's Wide Piazza

One of the last of Charleston's great antebellum houses to be built, 1 East Battery, looks seaward toward the stage upon which the Southern tragedy played its first act.

From its wide piazzas, South Carolinians cheered the arching fireball that burst over Fort Sumter April 12, 1861, to split the nation. Behind its shuttered windows four years later, sobered and saddened Charlestonians saw the first Yankee troops land in the city.

Between these dates, the house almost miraculously escaped serious damage from the Union artillery firing on the city from Morris Island. It was on the last day of Confederate occupation that the house received its first, and only, war wound.

A Major Bertody of a Georgia regiment was ordered to blow up a large Confederate cannon of English make that was mounted immediately in front of 1 East Battery. The gun was the largest owned by the Confederacy and it was considered impractical to move it.

The explosion sent pieces of the huge gun and carriage high into the air. One section of the carriage fell onto the roof of the house and was removed later when repairs were made. A segment of the barrel flew over this house and penetrated the roof of 9 East Battery where it still remains.

One of the house's better-known owners was Mrs. Mary Middleton Pinckney Lee, possessor of three of the South's proudest names.

She was a descendant of Henry I. Middleton, first president of the Continental Congress, and also of Arthur Middleton, signer of the Declaration of Independence.

Her first husband was Gustavus Memminger Pinckney of Charleston. After his death, she married Col. Robert E. Lee III, grandson of the Confederate leader. She is buried in Magnolia Cemetery between her two husbands.

Mrs. Lee was a great-granddaughter of Lt. Ralph Izard of Charleston who was a member of the desperate mission to burn the U.S. frigate *Philadelphia* which was held captive in the harbor of Tripoli in 1804. She also was a granddaughter of Christopher G. Memminger, first secretary of the Confederacy and a founder of Charleston's public school system.

The mansion was built about 1850 by Thomas A. Coffin, a member of a well-known Charleston and Beaufort clan. He sold it to Louis deSaussure in 1858 for $7,500 and the house still is called the deSaussure House although it was sold by that family in 1888.

The house occupies what is considered to be the most desirable location in the city. Its site gives it a commanding view of both the Cooper and Ashley Rivers, the entire harbor and the sea beyond.

1 East Battery — DeSaussure House looks out over harbor of history.

It was only a short distance from the site that the pirate Stede Bonnet and his men went to the gallows on White Point in 1718.

Their bodies hung from the gallows for a time as warning to those who might wish to fly the "Jolly Roger." Then they were buried below the high tide mark.

The South Carolina militia units that seized Fort Johnson and later fired the shot that began the Civil War boarded ship just up the harbor from this house. They passed off The Battery in the darkness en route across the harbor.

The house also witnessed the early trials of the Confederate submarine Hunley in 1863 and saw the first of the great United States 'Polaris submarines head oceanward on their undersea vigils in the atomic age.

As a modification of the classic single house, it has a main entrance on East Battery with a secondary entrance on its South Battery porch. The wrought iron window balconies are typical of those introduced by the architects of the day.

The house is solidly built of local brick with a stucco overlay and is dressed up by quoins. The interior ceilings are very tall and, despite the smallness of the lot, it gives the appearance of commanding a large space because of the open area surrounding it.

Bernard O'Neill purchased the house in 1888 and his family retained possession until 1926 when Mrs. Lee bought it. She sold it four years later to Arthur Barnwell of New York and Beaufort.

Mrs. Emily C. Ravenel and Mrs. Ruth C. Peeples came into possession in 1946 and sold it in 1950 to Ephriam Bril, a sometime Estonian export-import trader who converted it to apartments then suffered financial losses. W.D. Johnson of Tuscaloosa, Ala., bought the property in 1952. He sold it in 1959, and it is now owned by a group of three persons who hold it as a condominium.

Torpedo Boat Was Invented By Physician

The mansion at 5 East Battery was the home of a planter-scientist who turned his plowshares into a torpedo boat during the Civil War.

He was Dr. St. Julien Ravenel. It was due to his keenly inventive mind that the Confederate torpedo boat *David* was built at his Cooper River plantation, Stony Landing.

A more unlikely armament maker probably never lived. He studied medicine in Philadelphia and France. His wife was Harriet Horry Rutledge, and they had nine children. His father, John Ravenel, had built the house on East Battery about 1849. He had a large plantation, a substantial medical practice and had developed the first limestone mining works in the state on his plantation.

Dr. Ravenel developed a process for making phosphate rock readily soluble (and usuable as fertilizer). He produced an ammoniated fertilizer without use of ammonia. He developed the practice of adding marl to acid fertilizers to counteract free acid. He discovered the fact that planting and plowing-under of leguminous crops restored needed plant foods to the soil. He also was considered the "father" of Charleston's artesian water supply system. This, by eliminating the germ-laden shallow wells, saved thousands of lives.

he is best known, however, for his torpedo boat that attacked what was then the largest ironclad frigate in the world.

The cigar-shaped vessel, approximately 50 feet long and powered by a steam engine from a railroad shop, seriously damaged the Federal frigate *New Ironsides* off Charleston Harbor Oct. 5, 1863.

David Chenoweth Ebaugh, an engineer-lumberman, built the craft at Ravenel's suggestion. She was designed by him and built in a nitre shed at the plant at Stony Landing that he managed for the Confederate government. The craft was some five feet in diameter for 18 feet of its center, tapering gradually toward pointed ends.

A boiler was obtained at Fort Sumter and 18,000 pounds of iron ballast was placed in the *David's* bottom to steady the tricky vessel. In trial runs across the harbor, she cruised at 10 knots and Ebaugh turned her over to the Confederate Navy.

Ebaugh disagreed with the military (apparently correctly) over placement of an iron torpedo pole projecting from the bow of the vessel. He wrote later:

"They put it on an iron pipe about 2½ inches in diameter extending some 20-25 feet in front of the bow ... It was made stationary, the torpedo being some six feet under water. I had arranged it on bars of iron extending on both sides of the boat and hung on trunnions so as to raise it out of the water when the boat was in motion.

5 East Battery — Walls of Locally made brick are 32 inches thick.

Had they left my plan of carrying the torpedo, I have no doubt but they would have blown up the *Ironsides* as the torpedo would have been much deeper in the water."

The *David* steamed unnoticed through the blockading monitors off the harbor and ran directly at the *New Ironsides*. The torpedo hit her on the starboard side, near the engine room, about seven feet below the water line.

The explosion sent a sheet of water over the *David*, extinguishing the steam engine's fires. Two of the crew hung on to the craft as she drifted off in the darkness and managed to bring her back into the harbor after rekindling the fires. The other two were captured.

The *Ironsides* didn't sink, but she was badly damaged. What was more important, the gallant and dramatic attack helped dissuade the Northern Navy from attempting a frontal attack on the port of Charleston.

The *David* — and her successors — were not very successful. Ebaugh, for whom the semisubmersible was named, built other vessels at Stony Landing. One was a large vessel designed to run the blockade. She was captured in Charleston Harbor when the city was evacuated by the Confederates in 1865.

Dr. Ravenel and Theodore Stoney were partners in the Southern Torpedo Co. which backed the building of the *David*. Undoubtedly they and others met at 5 East Battery to discuss the vessel.

Dr. Ravenel's wife also was talented. She wrote the book, "Charleston, the Place and the People," which is one of the best characterizations of the city ever written.

The house was very nearly destroyed by the earthquake of 1886. The present simple cornices replaced the paneled cornices and urnlike ornaments originally gracing the eaves. This rebuilding job was accomplished by Harry Frost, Dr. Ravenel having died in 1882.

The front door is very handsome with hand-carved rosettes. The tiled vestibule opens onto a hall that affords a semicircular staircase along its northern wall. The hallway extends the length of the house with rooms between it and the portico.

The walls, undoubtedly of brick from a Cooper River kiln, perhaps one on a Ravenel holding, are 32 inches thick. Recessed paneling and a high chair rail decorate the second floor drawing room that permits a grand view of the harbor.

The house was bought from the Porcher family in 1953 by Dr. and Mrs. Joe Sam Palmer of Allendale.

Fragment Of Cannon Rests On Roof Beams

No. 9 East Battery is one of the few houses known to have a large fragment of a Civil War cannon resting in its attic, a fitting memento of the final days of the conflict. It also is a tribute to the solid construction of the 1838 mansion.

It was the first of the large houses to be built on that portion of East Battery, an area that was suspect because of its lowness and exposure to the devastating force of the hurricanes that occasionally batter the Lowcountry.

Its seemingly outsized colonnade was built both as a porch-roof support and as a bit of braggadocio, a monument to vanity — a soaring grouping of pillars to be admired from the distant reaches of the harbor and the Ashley River. These were the highways of the time, the avenues by which planters arrived in Charleston.

The Custis-Lee Mansion at Arlington was built with the same general idea. At close range, its portico looks bulky and even grossly brutal. Seen from across the Potomac, Arlington is in perspective. Robert William Roper's house at 9 East Battery was thus seen by its owners's peers, the tidewater planters, as their barges and 12-oared, cypress-tree boats approached Charleston.

The tall pillars and the handsome brick house with its crowning balustrade must have provided an imposing view from the water before the two existing houses were erected between it and South Battery.

Despite its grand appearance, No. 9 is, basically, a simple house, built purposely to produce a gracious style out of massiveness. The house is a large one and its proportions are in the grand style.

A porch was considered a necessity in the days when air conditioning was something that nature either provided or one did without. Unlike most Charleston houses, the Roper mansion's piazza arrangement has only two floors — the main one and the basement. The house roof and the porch roof are incoporated into a single unit, again "violating" the usual practice in houses of this period.

This diversity is probably attributable to the supposed architect for the building, Edward Brickell White, a designer of some note. No records exist to prove that he was the architect since his entire library was lost in the fire of 1861. However, the house bears his signature in many details.

Offsetting the simplicity and seriousness of its design, is the massive "rope"

"Rope" molding frames door.

moulding framing the entrance door. It has been intepreted as a pun on the name of the owner of the house. This sort of play is common in heraldry as "canting," a bit of decor that literally chants out the name of the possessor of a coat of arms, and it could well have been so devised in the Roper House doorway.

The hunk of cannon in the house attic landed there when Confederate forces were preparing to evacuate the city in February 1865, as Sherman's swift and pitiless marauders swung northward after the capture of Savannah. A Blakely cannon, weighing some 30 tons and one of the largest cannon in the Confederacy, was located in an earthwork at the corner of South and East Batteries. It could not be moved, so it was blown up. The explosion sent a huge fragment hurling high into the air and onto the roof of the Roper House.

The house's solid construction proved sufficient to the challenge. The heavy piece of iron penetrated the roof and came to rest on the attic floor. Later it was considered too heavy to risk on the stairs and so it remains there today, one of the best conversation "pieces" a house could hope to acquire.

The Charleston earthquake of 1886 gave the house another sort of testing. Again it stood firm against the great tremors that flattened many Charleston buildings and toppled the similary massive pillars of the Ravenel House at 13 East Battery.

While Roper's house received some cracked masonry, it did not fall. Following the earthquake, the house's owners had "earthquake rods" installed and, continuing the elegance of its builders, they covered the "washer" at street end of each rod with an ornate iron lion's head.

The house was the property of the Seigling family for many years. In 1929 it was sold by them to Solomon R. Guggenheim of the New York clan of multimillionaires and one of the oustanding patrons of modern art. Guggenheim's estate sold it to J. Drayton Hastie in 1952. In 1968 it was purchased from Hastie by Richard H. Jenrette, a New York investment banker.

The grounds once extended through to Church Street on the west. However, when Hastie purchased the property, he sold the Church Street portion of the holdings.

9 East Battery — Outsized colonnade was built as a bit of braggadocio.

Residence Built Before Civil War Lost Portico In 1886 Earthquake

The antebellum mansion at 13 East Battery literally lost its face in the earthquake of 1886 and saw a long-lost portion of its once massive portico uncovered by Hurricane Gracie in 1959.

When Charleston was shaken by the massive earthquake, the tall columns crumbled. The soaring roof of the porch, an extension of the main roof, remained cantilevered out over the arch-supported, first-floor piazza.

It was considered economically unfeasible to restore the pillars, what with the poverty of the former Confederate bastion following the Civil War, so the damaged porch roof section was taken off. The gable end was sealed with brick from the ruined columns and the big house has stood thus ever since.

When Hurricane Gracie brought 100-mile-an-hour winds to Charleston in 1959, one of the victims was a huge tree in the yard next door to 13 East Battery. The big tree toppled and its roots loosened the earth beneath it as they were forced up by the weight of the falling tree.

Workmen clearing the area discovered one of the capitals of the tall columns in the earth beneath the roots. Apparently the force of its fall in 1886 had driven the capital into the soft earth. Time and nature combined to cover it, and a tree grew over it, enclosing it with its roots.

13 East Battery is one of Charleston's tallest waterfront houses. Early in the morning of April 12, 1861, Charlestonians stood on its wide roof to watch the start of the Civil War. It apparently escaped injury during the Federal siege of Charleston. It also was not harmed when a huge Confederate cannon was blown up at the intersection of East and South Batteries while the Southern forces wre evacuating the city in 1865.

The explosion of the cannon sent a large fragment of its barrel through the roof of No. 9 East Battery, but No. 13 was not damaged.

The quoins at the corners and matching work on the first floor porch supporters were typical of 1845 when the house was built. Brick for its thick walls came from brickyards on Lowcountry rivers. Heart pine went into its sills and flooring and intricately designed ironwork adorns the balcony stretching across its front.

The house is a variation on the Charleston single-house pattern, necessarily so because its builder was faced with the problem of placing a mansion-sized dwelling on a lot whose narrowness better fitted it for a small cottage.

He achieved success by placing the entry at the street end, under the portico. Then he flanked it with a carriage entrance, also under the portico and beneath part of the house itself. The entry hall is a long one extending to the center of the

13 East Battery — One of Charleston's tallest waterfront houses.

house where a stair affords access to the upper floors.

The drawing room is one of the largest in the city, occupying the full width of the house. It has fireplaces at either end, and its windows provide magnificent views of the harbor. French windows lead to the piazza and to the third-floor balcony.

From the piazza one is able to see the full sweep of Charleston Harbor and its historic sites — Fort Sumter, Fort Moultrie, Fort Johnson, Castle Pinckney, Rebellion Roads, Morris Island and others.

During the era when Charleston's Negro street vendors pushed their carts along the streets to provide door delivery, residents of 13 East Battery used their own homemade elevator system.

A sturdy wicker basket would be lowered over the side of the big porch. Dickering for purchases was done from this superior height and then the produce-laden basket would be pulled up by rope.

The iron fence, gate posts and an iron ballustrade around the piazza all were destroyed in the earthquake.

The rear portion of the house is narrower than the front which occupies most of the lot's width. This back section consists of a long extension with narrow porches, the constriction of house space permitting a narrow side garden.

The carriage house at the rear of the lot has been converted into an attractive garden apartment.

The house is known as the William Ravenel House from its builders and long-time owners.

21 East Battery — Alston family coat of arms decorates parapet.

House Built On Site Of Fort

The house at 21 East Battery stands partially on the site of one of the earliest defenses of the city and was built by one of Charleston's most successful immigrant merchant princes.

Charles Edmondston left his native Scotland for the promise of riches in America and he found them. After purchasing a wharf site where Exchange Street now connects East Bay with the waterfront, Edmondston proceeded to accumulate a fortune.

In 1829 he built the spacious mansion that is now 21 East Battery. But fortune proved fickle and in 1839 his property was sold to satisfy creditors, his debts being estimated at $125,000 — a large amount at that time.

Charles Alston, who acquired the property then, was the distinguished son of a distinguished father, Col. William Alston of Waccamaw, one of the state's wealthiest planters. It was at Alston's house that George Washington stayed when he paused at Georgetown on his tour of the nation in 1791.

The family included Theodosia Burr Alston, daughter of Aaron Burr, wife of a state governor and victim of a tragic death at sea.

Alston built the parapet atop the house and placed his family coat of arms upon it, one of the few residences here to be decorated in such a manner. He also may have had the wrought iron fence, gate lantern and balcony installed. The fence and gates have been battered to the ground on at least two occasions by hurricane-tossed debris.

The house is partially on the site of Fort Mechanic, so-called because the "mechanics" (carpenters, etc.) of Charleston contributed their services free of charge to build it in 1795. The "state of war" with France was on and Charlestonians rallied to the still young and not-too-rich nation. An earlier fortification, Lyttleton's, or Middle Bastion, was in the area when the city's fortifications were extended more than a century prior to Edmonston's house building.

Through the dignified entrance door one enters a large hall extending across the northern side of the house and connecting with a side hall entrance that runs north-south across the house from the porch.

There are large rooms on either side of this hall from which a square-built stairway ascends to the second-floor drawing rooms.

These are "en suite" with large folding doors and may be opened to include the upper stair hall, making one large room. The plan insures coolness in summer and provides space for entertaining on a grand scale.

From the wide porches on the east balcony, a magnificent view of Charleston Harbor is achieved across the High Battery wall between street and water. This wall originally was of wood and sand, but repeated destruction by hurricanes caused the city fathers to begin a stone construction project in 1804. the ugly pipe railings now along East Battery replaced earlier wooden ones of cypress. These had handsome posts with carved acorn tops.

The house was the residence for may years of J.J. Pringle Smith, owner of Middleton Place Gardens. It later was inherited by his grandson, Charles H.P. Duell, and Mrs. Duell. The main house is operated by the Historic Charleston Foundation as a museum and is open to the public.

With its extensive outbuildings, handsome facade, wide piazzas and wrought iron fencing, the house is a grand example of the taste and affluence of the early 19th century.

37 Church — Charming residence has elements of Dutch architectural ancestry.

Gold Kept In Keg

Safe's Location Foiled Thieves

The house at 37 Church St. may have had one of the most unusual "bank vaults" of all time.

Legend has it that one of its early owners kept his money in a cask of water on the front stoop of the house, apparently relying on the theory that no one would try to steal a keg of water.

The house predates 1750 and may be quite a bit older. In 1692 the land on which it stands consisted of two lots which were granted to Mrs. Susannah Varin, a daughter of Samuel Horry, a leading Carolina Huguenot.

Mrs. Varin sold the property in 1695 to Major John Vanderhorst. This house, or more plausibly its predecessor, appears to have been occupied by a member of the Vanderhorst family prior to 1700. By 1750, however, it had been purchased by Anthony Matthews, an early settler who left a large and notable family.

In May, 1752, Lois Matthews, widow of Anthony, sold a portion of her Church Street property to George Everleigh, a prosperous Indian trader who built the house to the north, No. 39 Church.

George Matthews inherited No. 37 before 1759 and sold it to Dr. Philip Skirving 10 years later.

The square brick house has some elements of Dutch architectural ancestry, a decor that could have been implanted by the Vanderhorsts. At any rate, John Vanderhorst appears to have been engaged in a fairly lucrative sea trade, owning his own ships and plying between Charleston and the West Indies.

It was this salty old captain who reportedly kept his gold coins hidden in the water cask in full view of passersby.

When the nature of the "bank" was disclosed, a local wag is supposed to have remarked that no one in his right mind would ever steal a keg of water, and the old captain never drank water so the gold was safe.

The present double piazzas probably were added after the house was built. With its "bell" roof (the slope shapes upward, like the lip of a bell, near the eaves to send rainfall cascading away from the walls) a half-bullseye on the east and a dormer

above the piazzas, the house is one of the most charming in the city.

When the house was built, it fronted on a small marsh gutter, called Vanderhorst Creek, that penetrated the Charleston peninsula just south of the walled town, where Water Street is today.

An arm of the creek extended south where Church Street makes a bend today. Farther south, the street commenced again and was known as "Church Street Extended" for many years until Vanderhorst Creek was filled and became a roadbed.

The property was owned by Martin W. Stobo in 1816 when it was bought by Thomas Hall Jervey. In 1863 it was sold to Theodore DeHon Jervey by H.D. Lesesne who was acting as a trustee in a postnuptial marriage settlement between John Laurens and his wife, Eliza R. Laurens.

A Charleston harbor pilot, S.S. Hancock, bought the house in 1867 and sold it 20 years later to Roswell T. Logan and it has remained in the Logan family.

Merchant Built On 1692 Grant

For more than two centuries this charming little early Georgian house has looked out from its picturesque vantage point in the bend of Church Street.

Moil of war and brine of sea have swirled past its window shutters. Lovers of old and those of the space age have paused on moon-speckled pavement beneath the oaks to view its serene facade.

The house at 39 Church St. played its role in the develpment of Charleston, its builder, George Eveleigh, being one of the great merchants who helped open the hinterlands. He had a store at Augusta to which he sent British goods for the widening frontier in Cherokee country and from which came pack trains with skins for shipment to England.

Behind its massive front door rests a Civil War cannon ball. The large, solid ball was picked up near East Battery by R.M. Marshall whose family subsequently purchased the Eveleigh residence. Beside it is a smaller shot of Revolutionary War vintage dug up on the premises.

Past this house on the night of Sept. 14, 1775, fled the last royal governor of Carolina, Sir William Campbell. His precipitate departure from 34 Meeting St. (immediately behind Eveleigh's house) was to unite wavering Charlestonians into a solid force against the British. Campbell boarded a small boat in the marshes then existing north of 39 Church and escaped to a British warship in the lower harbor.

The house at that time was owned by Mrs. Daniel Blake who also owned 34 Meeting. The land grant dates back to 1692. When the French Revolution sent many refugees abroad, one of the more prominent emigres was Dr. Jean Louis Polony, who came to Charleston from Santo Domingo. He bought the house and lived there for awhile, continuing his medical practice and also research in botany.

A handsome wrought iron gate in a high, stucco-over-brick wall leads through a shallow front yard to the flagstoned porch. Unlike most old Charleston houses, it is built low to the ground. The original brick porch pillars were lost in the great hurricane of 1752. That storm swept Charleston Harbor clear of ships, driving one of nine-feet draft up a creek that flowed where Water Street now is located, grounding her well up on Church Street.

Except for minor interior changes, the house is structurally the same as when Eveleigh built it. Two small rear rooms on the ground floor have been combined to create a large dining room. Miss May O. Marshall installed Adam mantels, taken from the East Bay town house of Nathaniel Heyward after it was partially destroyed.

The second floor has a drawing room extending the width of the house behind the piazza. One of the Heyward house mantels in in this room. It is unusally wide

39 Church — Georgian house is one of the most photographed in the city.

and depicts a fox hunt in its central panel. Slender colonettes support either side with a Greek muse above and sheep in the arch over her head. The room is paneled with wide, beveled cypress panels.

The mantel replaces a marble one broken in the earthquake of 1886.

The house was unroofed by a tornado in 1811. The whirling winds lifted one of the roof beams from the house and drove it through the roof of a residence on King Street, two blocks west.

The Marshall family obtained the house in 1875 and it has remained in the family. The Marshall who bought it was a son of the Rev. Dr. Alexander W. Marshall, rector of St. John's Episcopal Chapel during the last months of the Civil War. Dr. Marshall refused to use the Episcopal prayer, "for the President of the United States,"

because of its political nature. Immediately after Lee's surrender, Dr. Marshall was banished from the city by U.S. Gen. John P. Hatch. His personal property also was ordered confiscated. He returned to Charleston in the late 1860s.

The garden contains one of the city's largest magnolia trees. An outbuilding extends along the northern wall of the property at the rear. In front, along the curve of the sidewalk, are four sandstone posts. Four large oaks shade the brick paved street that curves gently northeastward at that point.

The symmetry of its facade, its picturesque setting and the softly curving brick-paved street combine to make the house one of the most photographed residences in the city.

Physician Died For Love

Rue should grow in the old-fashioned garden of the house at 59 Church St. where a 22-year-old man died for love more than 200 years ago.

He was Dr. Joseph Ladd Brown, late of Rhode Island, medical doctor by vocation, poet by avocation and loser in a duel over an actress.

His ghost is said to still haunt the lovely old house that was built by Thomas Rose about 1732. It is a charming building in the early Georgian manner and much more commodious than its street facade would indicate.

Rose apparently built the house shortly after he married Beuler Elliott who inherited the land from her father. The Elliotts were a very well-to-do family. They also were very pious, a factor that went a bit against the grain of the Cavalier types who constituted the majority of Charleston's citizenry in the early 18th century.

One of her brothers, for instance, donated the land immediately to the north to a group of Maine Baptists who fled that rock-bound coast and its puritanical religious leaders because of a theological difference of opinion concerning infant baptism. With their pastor they sought haven in Charleston and received it. So numerous did they become in the southern stretch of Church Street that it obtained the epithet of "Baptist Town."

Mrs. Rose's relatives subsequently helped establish a rival Baptist Church a few doors south on the opposite side of Church Street. The building — a wooden one — stood until well after 1900 when it was demolished. The older Baptist church, "mother church" of Southern Baptists, is still standing.

The Rose family sold 59 Church St. to the Savage family in 1741. This clan was to occupy it for 95 years and to witness its safe passage through the Revolution. When built, the house had a central door from the street directly into the very large downstairs parlor. In its early days, this room probably was a business office of sorts. Today, five windows penetrate the wide facade, giving light to the room and balance to the building.

The upstairs drawing room also had a central door. It opened onto a balcony over the sidewalk. The house was built during the second decade of Royal rule of Carolina, an era that brought great prosperity to the Colonials, something they had not experienced under the quarrelsome rule of the Lords Proprietor.

Church Street was well within the walls of Old Charles Towne and its fairly high elevation above tidewater gave it some protection against hurricanes. One memorable storm sent a schooner of 9-foot draft up Church Street, very near to the front door of No. 59. The stoutly-built house stood against the onslaught of nature as in future years it was to withstand the earthquake of 1886 and the always present destructive hand of man.

The house passed from the Savage family in the 1830s and subsequently had a number of owners. It was restored in 1929 by the Frank E. Whitmans who added the piazzas and gateway at that time. Mr. and Mrs. Henry Staats bought it in 1941. Later they purchased a house to the south, razed it, and created the lovely garden that so delights visitors today.

The house, with its background of piety and prosperous tranquility, became the center of one of Charleston's most romantic duels.

The year was 1786 and young Dr. Brown was practicing medicine in Charleston and writing poetry as a hobby. Like most young bachelors of the day, he attended the theater and had become fast friends with another young man, Ralph Isaacs.

Then a Miss Barrett came to town, acting in the production of Shakespeare's Richard III. Brown lost his heart. Isaacs thought the actress — nicknamed "Perdita" because of a fancied likeness to the English actress of that name — was only so-so.

They argued. The debate finally reached the stage where they were writing letters to the newspapers criticizing each other's opinions and ultimately to a duel.

Dr. Brown apparently fired into the air, but Isaacs, hoping to give his opponent a flesh wound, aimed for the legs. His aim was not good and Dr. Brown received a serious wound. He was taken to 59 Chruch where he died three weeks later. Perdita and the theatrical cast had left town and the young lover died without a parting farewell from the object of his affections.

The old house stands today, the churchyard to the north filled with long dead and pious Baptists. In its upper rooms, the ghost of a cavalier poet also is silent.

59 Church — House was built in 1732 in a section of the city that in those days was known as "Baptist Town."

Second Floor Drawing Room One Of Handsomest In City

Ever since its construction about 1745, the handsome house at 69 Church St. has been associated with families prominent in the city, state and nation. From it have come men and women who contributed greatly to the literary, art and government life of the area.

It is one of the city's largest private houses and its second-story drawing room, spanning the width of the dwelling, is among the handsomest and most spacious in Charleston.

Rebecca Brewton Motte, the heroine of Fort Motte, grew up next door, at 71 Church St., and married Jacob Motte, the younger, who lived here. Col. Motte, senior, was the public treasurer of the Royal Colony for 27 years and occupied No. 69 as a residence although he was not the owner.

It was owned by the William Mason Smith family from 1869 until the 1960s when it was purchased by Anthony Cecil. He had the south piazzas removed and restored the central front door and hall on the street side.

In 1869 the house was in very sad shape having been hit by several shells during the Civil War.

Mrs. William Mason Smith, Sr., carefully restored the mansion. Left a widow at 25 with five children, she conducted a school in the big house.

Richard Capers, its builder, was head of a family that was to give South Carolina three Episcopal bishops, one of whom was a brigadier general in the Confederate Army before donning the robes of a cleric.

A progenitor of the Smith family was South Carolina's first Episcopal bishop, the Right Rev. Robert Smith. During the years of Smith occupancy, the house contained his breakfront and a part of his library as well as an oil painting of the bishop that is somewhat of a family controversy. It is one of two or three that appear to be exactly alike and it depends on which branch of the family is present to decide which painting is the original.

In more recent years, the house was owned by Daniel Elliott Huger Smith. With his daughter, Alice Ravenel Huger Smith, he wrote "The Dwelling Houses of Charleston," a definitive history of the city's old houses that also contains a pot pourri of historical items concerning their inhabitants.

Miss Smith became one of the city's best known artists and her paintings were exhibited widely. They are in great demand today because of the soft sentimentality and remarkable integrity with which she captured the feel of the Lowcountry.

Rebecca Brewton Motte was refugeeing at the Motte plantation on the Congaree River when the main house was seized by the British Army and fortified. When Col. Henry Lee and Gen Francis Marion arrived to attack the Redcoats, Mrs. Motte

69 Church — Residence is one of Charleston's largest.

herself gave the order to set her home afire, even providing the arrows with which the act was accomplished.

The Motte family sold the Church Street house to Col. James Parsons in 1778. He had a great record as a soldier in the Revolution and also was a member of the Continental Congress. He was offered the vice presidency of South Carolina in 1776 but turned it down.

A wealthy planter and merchant, O'Brien Smith, bought the property in 1800 and kept it for 11 years. It was possibly this Smith who installed the beautiful Adam mantels that now grace the big fireplaces. He also seems to have been responsible for creating the handsome drawing room by making a wide arched opening between the two street-front rooms on the second floor.

Smith also closed the central door on the street that formerly opened into the room that is now a dining room. It was obviously an office prior to his alterations, the house being typical of the sort built by merchants of the pre-Revolutionary period.

The house is unusual also in that it has

a full cellar, an adjunct not normal to the houses built on the low-lying Charleston peninsula. Its upper rooms have the same tall ceilings as the ground floor. With its attic and cellar, it has a total of five floors.

Like the main house, a charming outbuilding at the rear is built of Lowcountry brick. This former kitchen and servant facility has windows with pointed arches, an architectural departure from the normal style of houses of the period.

The house has a large lot and a rear entrance on Ford Court which gives it access to Meeting Street on the west.

Its position, atop a rise of ground running back from the Cooper River waterfront, and the fact that its first floor is about three feet above ground level undoubtely has stood it well during hurricanes.

One storm drove a schooner of nine-foot draft up Water Street and into Church Street, a scant half-block south. But the house at No. 69 withstood the winds and the waters.

Its windows look out onto a walled garden at the rear.

Woman Paid Penalty For Nimble Wit

The spirited woman who once owned the house at 71 Church St. talked back to a British officer — and was banished to Philadelphia for her nimble wit and sharp tongue.

He was Lt. Col. Banastre Tarleton. She was Mary Weyman Brewton Foster. It was 1781. Tarleton, one of the most daring of the British cavalry leaders, was still smarting from a disastrous whipping administered to him at Cowpens by Charleston's Col. William Washington, a cousin of the more famous George Washington.

Charleston had fallen and the British were masters of the area. At a reception, Tarleton, a pink-cheeked and dandyish officer, was piqued by hearing Charlestonians speaking admiringly of the feats of Col. Washington.

Said the lieutenant colonel: "I would like to see this fellow Washington of whom you people talk so much."

Whereupon Mrs. Foster retorted: "What a pity you did not look behind you at the battle of Cowpens."

Her first husband had been John Brewton who had left her the house at 71 Church. Her audacity went well with the Brewton family which had produced a number of fire-eaters, including Rebecca Brewton Motte. That vivacious lady helped the Patriots burn her own house in order to evict British troops who had turned it into a fortification, known as Fort Motte.

The Brewtons got the Church Street property in 1716 and it's fairly certain there were no buildings of any substance on the lot at that time. It was a part of Lot No. 57 on the Grand Modell of Charles Towne. John Cock — or Cook — a mariner, bought it April 30, 1701, from William Welsby, a butcher. Cock left it to the children of his two sisters, Hannah Martin and Katherine Welsby. Cock's executors sold it to Michael (Miles) Brewton who lived just to the north at what is now 73 Church St.

Brewton is listed as a goldsmith, which meant that he also was a banker and moneylender of sorts. He subsequently transferred 73 Church to a daughter, Mary Dale. This transaction identifies his son, Robert Brewton, as living on the northern portion of Lot 57. It also provided for a three-foot-wide alley to be kept open at all times between the two houses. The right-of-way was mentioned in later property transfers, but the alley apparently was closed during the 1880-1942 period when it was owned by the Huger and Kershaw families.

Robert Brewton sold 71 Church to his sister and brother-in-law, Rebecca and Jordan Roche, in 1745.

71 Church — House is prototype of hundreds that line Charleston streets.

When Roche died, he left no will. His heir at law was a brother, Francis Roche, who conveyed the property by deed to Rebecca Roche and also life interest in other properties.

In those days women were not allowed to control real estate very often, so Mrs. Roche married again, very quickly, to one James Guthrie. She also died without a will and her heir at law was Robert Brewton Jr., a nephew who lived in Philadelphia.

His son, John Brewton, married pretty Mary Weyman in 1771 and died in 1777. She then married Thomas Foster and was his wife when she crossed words with Tarleton.

The Brewtons sold the property to John Mitchell who conveyed it to Samuel Prioleau, a worthy patriot of the Revolution. Adam Gilchrist bought it from Prioleau in 1814. Other owners and dates of purchase include Mary M. Faber, 1822; D.G. Joye, 1847; C.N. Spratt, 1852; Francis C. Black, 1879; and Mrs. Margaret C. Huger, 1880.

It is Charleston's oldest single house, the prototype of hundreds that stand along the town's streets, their ends to the sidewalk, their porches to the south or west and their north walls windowless or nearly so. The latter kept out the cold northern and easterly winds of winter. It also gave the next door neighbor privacy in his garden.

No. 71 Church has very thick brick walls with heavy cornices under the eaves formed by specially shaped local brick.

Bedpost Partly Supports Floor

George Washington probably addressed the people of Charleston in 1791 from the balcony of the house at 78 Church St.

And — although it had nothing to do with the nation's first president — the third floor of the house is partially supported by an antique mahogany bedpost. A contractor found it when the house was being renovated several years ago. It was behind an old plaster wall where it remains today, proof of the "make-do" adaptability of Charlestonians that has served them so well in times of disaster.

The first president was staying at the Heyward-Washington House, a block to the north. Legend has it that he was asked to speak to a large gathering of Charlestonians assembled before his temporary residence.

He resolved the matter of an elevated platform by crossing the street and mounting the balcony of No. 78 Church, whence he spoke. History does not record the act, but the house was there at the time and its balcony does afford a commanding eminence for a speaker.

During the 1920s the tiny adjunct to the south, now 76 Church, was the residence of Charleston author and playwright DuBose Heyward who wrote the immortal story of "Porgy." Later this was to become "Porgy and Bess." Up the street, a tenement next door to the house Washington stayed in was to become famous as "Catfish Row."

The fact that it was actually "Cabbage Row," and two blocks removed from Heyward's locale for Catfish Row, doesn't change what has become local legend.

Some years ago 76 and 78 Church St. were restored and converted back to single-family status by the J. Ross Hanahans after long years of existence as apartment units.

Each of the houses is old, dating certainly to the post-Revolutionary period and perhaps earlier. The quaintness of the pair makes them a most attractive part of the charm that is Church Street.

The larger, No. 78, also has the distinction of being quite different from its Charleston neighbors of the same era. Its builder is not known, but the architectural style hints at someone from Virginia or New England. With its end chimneys rising wide above the roofridge, the house has the characteristics of the much larger Tidewater Virginia plantation mansions. Its low ceilings smack of New Engalnd. In Charleston, most houses tended to have the chimneys in the center, rather than at the ends. In the case of the usual Charleston single house, the chimneys were on the north or east side.

While the house apparently was smaller when built, it has seen additions that have greatly increased its living area. Before the extensive restoration accomplished by the Hanahans, tiles on a small shed roof were of a type used in very early construction in Charleston.

Another departure from the Charleston norm is the fact that the house has a cellar. This was permissable only because the elevation of the land at that point is well above the reach of high tide. The cellar actually extends beyond the house and under the sidewalk, a fact that could indicate it was part of an earlier construction.

Harold Tatum, a Charleston archictect, said the house at 78 Church appears to have had a spiral staircase when built. This would explain the narrowness of the stair hall and the unusual two-way steps leading to the third floor.

The balcony of old iron affords a spectacularly beautiful view of St. Philip's Church farther up the street, a view usually impossible from pedestrian level because of parked cars.

The houses have had many owners. Prior to World War I, Mr. and Mrs. Henry Whilden owned the house at No. 78 Church. Mrs. Hanahan, a niece of Mrs. Whilden, obtained the house after her aunt's death.

78 Church — Washington may have spoken from balcony.

87 Church — President Washington stayed here in 1791.

Heyward-Washington House One Of Nation's Most Historic

The Pre-Revolutionary War residence at 87 Church St. is one of the more historic houses of America, the home of a signer of the Declaration of Independence and a temporary residence for the nation's first president, George Washington.

Thomas Heyward, one of the four Declaration of Independence signers from South Carolina, inherited the colonial mansion from his father, Daniel Heyward, a wealthy planter who built the residence about 1770.

The house was turned over to President Washington when he visited Charleston in 1791 during his state tour of the nation. At that time, it was in the center of the city's finest residential area.

The residence also is of historic significance in the historic preservation movement, being the first dwelling to be restored and operated as a house museum. It is owned by the Charleston Museum and is open to the public.

The Museum was assisted in the restoration by the Society for the Preservation of Old Dwellings, now called the Charleston Preservation Society. The Museum ac-

quired the property in 1929 when the house had become a slum and was about to be demolished.

The preservationists raised funds by organizing house and plantation tours, musicals and other benefit events. The architectural firm of Simons and Lapham was retained for the restoration work.

On July 26, 1770, the South Carolina Gazette carried an advertisement announcing the pending sale of the Church Street lot at auction by the Provost Marshal under order of the South Carolina Court of Common Pleas. The advertisement said, in part: "On the said lot is a good brick house, two Stories high with other convenient buildings."

At the auction, Daniel Heyward Esq., "of the Euhaws," submitted the highest bid, 5,500 pounds "lawful current money of the province." The title deed was conveyed to him Aug. 1, 1770.

Heyward demolished the two-story dwelling and replaced it with the present three-story structure. It is not clear whether he retained any of the outbuildings.

The dwelling, a double-house with four rooms to the floor and a central stairhall, is similar in many ways to other houses built in the city during the rather prosperous era preceding the Revolution.

The exterior is of "Charleston Gray Brick," an oversized and unglazed brick that was made and sun-dried at brickyards along the state's tidewater rivers. The brick are laid in Flemish bond, a pattern rather popular in the Lowcountry.

A full half-story attic occupies the fourth floor which is covered by a slate hip roof.

Interiors are in the elaborate Georgian style popular at the time. The exterior is somewhat vertical in emphasis, a forerunner of the Adamesque and Federal architectural styles that burgeoned following the Revolution. The drawing room, with a trio of windows looking out on Church Street, is fully paneled. Doorways have broken pediments and eared surrounds. The mantel is attributed to Thomas Elfe, a local cabinetmaker, whose workshop, "The Thomas Elfe House," stands at 54 Queen Street a few blocks away.

The mantel has elaborate consoles, dentil courses and fretwork reminiscent of the style of Thomas Chippendale, the English furniture builder.

The frame of the overmantel bears a band of mahogany fretwork on a smaller scale and there is a fretwork band in the room's deep, coved cornice.

There are four chimneys. The fireplace walls of the other rooms are paneled with simpler mantels and cornices.

The staircase has mahogany handrails and a paneled enclosure.

Daniel Heyward died in 1777 and left the property to his widow for use during her lifetime. Their son, Thomas Heyward, later assumed ownership.

The Heyward family was one of the Lowcountry's wealthiest and most powerful families, owning many plantations and a great deal of city property. Thomas Heyward maintained the house as a fully-furnished town house and rented it to the City of Charleston for use by President Washington. In 1794, Heyward sold the property to John F. Grimke, a member of another wealthy plantation clan.

It subsequently changed hands a number of times and had its southeast front room converted into a bakery with a Victorian style store front. Architect Albert Simons had to design a new front entry and later, when a pre-bakery era photograph was found, it was discovered that the door designed by Simons was almost identical to the original.

Following the Civil War, the house, and many of its neighbors, deteriorated to slum status and became a tenement.

Behind the house lie the garden and outbuildings, one of these being the "cook house" which, the settlers learned early, must be kept separate from the main house due to the danger of fire.

The garden was restored under the direction of the late Emma B. Richardson, assistant director of the Museum, who collected such plants as would have adorned a late 18th century Charleston garden designed to provide flowers, herbs and "garden sass."

Nonexistent Catfish Row Lives Today

Like Sherlock Holmes' nonexistent home at "221-B Baker St." and Juliet's balcony in Verona, Charleston's "Catfish Row" never was, but is.

The ghosts of Porgy and Bess haunt the old tenement at 89-91 Church St. just as effectively as if they were real creatures.

A swank shop now entices the passerby to buy items where rows of cabbage used to grace the former vegetable stalls, giving the place its name of "Cabbage Row."

The metamorphosis from cabbage to catfish was accomplished by the clever pen of DuBose Heyward. It was his "Porgy" and its musical version, "Porgy and Bess," that drew worldwide attention to Charleston.

But Heyward's Catfish Row was a water-front tenement and the Cabbage Row, where the real Porgy had at least a "sometimey" residence, was at 89-91 Church St. Heyward simply moved the tenement two blocks eastward to Vanderhorst's Wharf to provide the waterfront locale necessary to his story.

But legend — just as remorselessly — moved it back to the west side of Church Street and it seems to have been a happy transition.

Heyward wrote "Porgy" and then collaborated with George Gershwin to produce the folk opera "Porgy and Bess."

The crippled beggar, Goat Cart Sammy, who was Heyward's pattern for the fictional Porgy, lived a life that was about as hauntingly and sadly lovely as did his more glamorous image in the opera.

He was Sammy Smalls and Charlestonians who remembered him recalled that he drove a goat-drawn cart with a small platform just clearing its four small iron wheels. He held out a tin drinking cup while begging for coins from passersby.

The late Maj. Henry F. Church sketched the ill-smelling cripple and goat while Sammy was copping a few pennies beneath Church's office window. This may be the only real-life record of Sammy, and it was insured for thousands of dollars when it hung in the sacrosanct halls of Milan's La Scala opera house when "Porgy and Bess" was presented there.

While Porgy achieved immortality in afterlife, the real Sammy compiled an enviable stock of police citations while alive. The records showed that he shot at least two women, neither of them Bess.

He shot at many others, but apparently was a very poor marksman. On one occasion, however, he was credited with putting two bullets into the rib cage of Sally Singleton.

His last offense — of record — was a one-shot attack on Maggie Barnes.

That was shortly after World War I. Then Goat Cart Sammy disappeared from Charleston. Broad Street saw him no more and all save a few devoted white friends

89-91 Church — Vegetable stalls once graced tenement's exterior.

forgot the antagonistic black beggar with the winsome face.

Five years passed and Maj. Church decided to find out what had happened to Sammy. He enlisted the aid of Charleston's Detective Chief John J. Healy. That doughty Irishman painstakingly ferreted through the hundreds of Negroes named Smalls in Charleston until he found that Goat Cart Sammy had gone to "Jim" Island.

James Island then was a farming community with blacks outnumbering whites six to one. The trail led down narrow dirt roads and hardpacked paths between the "hopping john" patches of okra, cowpeas and garden sass to a small clapboard shack near the salt marshes.

And to the real Bess.

Only her name was Normie. It was she — the everloving wife — who took Porgy back after disease and time had made its inroads into his frail body. It was Normie who walked alongside the rickety, iron-wheeled cart as it made its way westward across the then new Ashley River Bridge and then southward onto the sea island.

And it was Normie who laid her man to rest outside a small graveyard in the "Jim" Island woodlands. Porgy was buried "crossways of the world" (North-South rather than East-West) because he died as he lived, unrepentant. She told Maj. Church that the goat died shortly after Sammy. "He didn't eat nothin' after Sammy gone. He just grieve and die. He want to be wid Sammy," she said.

And Normie set the record straight on Sammy's shooting scrapes — particularly insofar as Heyward's theme that Porgy shot Bess in the skirt because he loved her.

"Please, suh," she asked, "if they write any more 'bout Sammy, please tell 'em Sammy ain't shoot de woman in the skirt cause he love her. He shoot her cause he thought she stole his wrist watch.

Actually, Heyward didn't know there was a real-life Bess and his development of Porgy as a character was largely based on a composite. Heyward had worked with Charleston's waterfront longshoremen and dock wallopers and he put the facets of many into the frail body that became Porgy.

In 1986 a proper gravestone was placed at Porgy's grave.

The building at 89-91 Church St. is a rather typical tenement. This term — now derogatory — simply meant rental property when this house was built sometime before the Revolutionary War. It escaped the disastrous fire of 1780 and survived the earthquake of 1886.

By 1888 the tenement had become a bordello frequented by sailors from the nearby waterfront. By 1900 it was inhabited by approximately 100 Negroes.

Some operated vegetable stalls and the orderly rows of cabbages in slanted bins along the street were depicted by artists and remain as proof of the origin of Cabbage Row.

It remained a slum until the 1920s when Loutrel W. Briggs, a landscape architect, came to Charleston. He bought the place, evicted its inhabitants and restored it.

The once handsome mantels and woodwork had long since gone "up the chimney" in the smoke of fires and Briggs bought woodwork from other old buildings to match the antiquity of the place.

He sold it in 1945 and it became a rental property.

House Witnessed Start Of Nullification Effort

The house at 94 Church St. was occupied by one of America's most tragic women. It also was the planning site of one of the nation's most tragic political movements.

It was the town house of Gov. Joseph Alston, husband of Theodosia Burr Alston who sailed from their plantation home at Georgetown into legendary oblivion. It was the meeting place of the organizers of the Nullification Movement of 1832 with John C. Calhoun leading the discussions in the second floor drawing room.

No. 94 Church is the northernmost of three houses that portray more than a half-century in the evolution of the Charleston single house. Its 1730 date is three decades ahead of No. 90. The house at No. 92 was built about 1809 in the former garden of its northerly neighbor.

While similar in general plan, each has its own distinctive window and door housings, ceiling heights, style of cornices and other decorative items. The house at 94 Church, while the oldest of the trio, has porches that were added after No. 90 was built, perhaps as an early 19th century attempt to "keep up with the Joneses."

Thomas Bee built the house at No. 94, launching from it a distinguished career following graduation from Oxford. He was a leader in the Colonial government after 1762 and one of the leaders of the Revolution. He was a delegate to the First and Second Continental Congresses (1775-76) and a member of the S.C. House of Representatives from 1776 to 1782, serving as speaker 1777-79.

He continued his civic and political activities while participating in military campaigns during the war and was a member of the Continental Congress from 1780 to 1782, moving to that post from the lieutenant governorship he held in 1779-80.

He was appointed U.S. District Judge for South Carolina in 1790 by George Washington. His grandson, Gen. Bernard

Fire plate beneath window.

Bee, was credited with labeling Gen. T.J. Jackson with the nickname "Stonewall" during the Civil War.

The house passed into the very wealthy Alston family of Waccamaw River. Gov. Joseph Alston came into its ownership some years before the tragic loss of his wife at sea.

She was Theodosia Burr, lovely and talented daughter of Aaron Burr. When her father returned from Europe in 1812, she decided to visit him. Her only child, Aaron Burr Alston had died in June and she was very unhappy. She sailed from Winyah Bay Dec. 30, 1812, aboard the schooner *Patriot*. Neither she nor the ship was ever heard from again.

In 1832 the house was the property of Alexander Christie's family. It was Christie who built the house to the south in 1809 after purchasing the Alston residence.

The Nullification Movement that eventually split the nation and — in some ways — led to the Civil War, started here. It was the most exciting thing to happen in Charleston since the Revolution. The papers probably were signed in the drawing room on the second floor, a room from which may be seen the historic Heyward-Washington House across the way and where the chimes of old St. Michael's Protestant Episcopal Church may be heard.

Calhoun, S.C. Gov. Robert Hayne, Gen. James Hamilton and other leaders of the movement deliberated here many days before the final draft of the Nullification Papers were signed.

The plan was aimed at defeating a tariff bill sponsored by congressmen from Northern industrial states that placed a heavy duty on such items as coarse woolens, cotton goods, iron and salt — items that the South needed but did not produce.

These Charlestonians believed in free trade and states' rights. They became known as Nullifiers and their opponents labeled them "Fire Eaters." That they failed in their efforts is history.

The bitterness engendered by the great Nullification debates created a schism that never was closed and which eventually broadened into the situation that ended with the firing on Fort Sumter nearly three decades later.

The house was bought in 1884 by George Paul. It was extensively renovated in the 1960s by one of his descendants, Dr. John R. Paul, and has since passed out of the family.

94 Church — John C. Calhoun led discussions in second floor room.

J.L. Petigru, A Study In Integrity

The house at 8 St. Michael's Alley could well be described in one sentence: "Here lived a man."

The house has notable architectural design and charm. But it is the strength, the personality and the plain bone-bred obstinance of James Louis Petigru that make his former law office especially important to Charleston's heritage of historic buildings.

Less than 100 feet away, in St. Michael's Protestant Episcopal Churchyard, stands the tombstone that records for all time Petigru's dedication to his ideals. At the same time, it describes the tolerance of antebellum Charleston that respected those beliefs although they were exactly opposite the Confederacy's cause.

No. 8 St. Michael's Alley was primarily Petigru's law office. However, he might have occupied it as a residence following the burning of his home at 129 Broad St. in the fire of 1861.

The handsome building with its wrought iron balcony was built in 1848. The property includes a garden with a charming small brick outbuilding that has been turned into arental unit. The buildings had fallen into disrepair by 1900 and the alley became a slum. Its houses were restored after 1915 when Miss Susan P. Frost purchased the row of former law offices on the alley's north side.

The house has beautiful woodwork and mantels, fortunately not destroyed during the slum period from the Reconstruction era until World War I.

Petigru's story is perhaps the greatest single refutation of the old canards that still crop up about Charleston and Charlestonians as intolerant, narrow-minded, clannish, hateful, snobbish, etc. For here was an Upcountryman — born on a farm in the flatwood section of Abbeville County — unallied with Charleston's "old" families and, moreover, a Unionist who opposed secession and a constitutionalist who opposed nullification. He also disliked slavery but was not an abolititionist. Negro slaves worked his family's home, Badwell, in Abbeville County and helped plant the white oak avenue that Pettigru himself laid out in the 1850s.

He was a leader of the Unionist Party and had a devastating wit that enabled him to tweak the noses of the great and pull the whiskers of his opposition without inviting hatred.

He was one of the strongest opposers of John C. Calhoun's nullification program. Ironically, Calhoun, a native of Edgefield which bordered Abbeville, was only a few years ahead of Petigru at the Classical Academy of Dr. Moses Waddel in Edgefield District. However, Calhoun — the Great Nullificationist — attended a Yankee school (Yale) while Petigru — the Unionist — graduated in 1812 with highest honors from South Carolina College, now the University of South Carolina.

He taught school and practiced law in Beaufort for several years before moving to Charleston in 1819. Here he soon became recognized as a lawyer of unusual ability, a gentleman of noble character and a great wit. He was the acknowledged leader of the Charleston Bar in 1830 when he openly opposed the nullification idea and from then — until his death 33 years later — he was to speak out strongly against the tenets held most sacred by his friends and neighbors.

But he kept his sense of humor to the last. In December, 1860, the Secession Convention convened in the Baptist Church at Columbia. A stranger asked Petigru the location of the insane asylum. The anti-secessionist leader silently raised his cane and pointed toward the church.

Petigru opposed nullification, stating he could find no justification for it in "law, logic or morals." Once he wrote an acquaintance: "I am devilishly puzzled to know whether my friends are mad, or I beside myself."

When he died March 9, 1863, the Civil War was at its height but Charleston remembered the man. The following day the city literally closed down for his funeral. The speakers were not his political friends, but his political enemies who took turns to eulogize in death the man they opposed in life.

His tombstone bears an epitaph so impressive that President Woodrow Wilson, attending the Paris Peace Conference in 1919, requested it be sent to him. The simple marble headstone bears these words:

8 St. Michael's Alley — Unionist lawyer's office.

JAMES LOUIS PETIGRU

"Born at Abbeville, May 10th, 1789. Died at Charleston March 9th, 1863. Jurist, Orator, Statesman, Patriot.

"Future times will hardly know how great a life this simple stone commemorates.

The tradition of his Eloquence, his Wisdom and his Wit may fade; But he lived for ends more durable than fame. His Eloquence was the protection of the poor and wronged; His Learning illuminated the principles of Law.

"In the admiration of his Peers, In the respect of his People, In the affection of his Family, His was the highest place; The just meed of his kindness and forbearance, His brilliant genius and his unwearied industry.

"Unawed by Opinion, Unseduced by Flattery, Undismayed by Disaster, He confronted life with an antique courage and Death with Christian Hope.

"In the great Civil War, He withstood his people for his Country, But his People did homage to the man who held his conscience higher than their praise; And his country Heaped her honors on the living, His own righteous self-respect sufficed Alike for Motive and Reward.

"Nothing is here for tears, nothing to wail or knock the breast; no weakness, no contempt, Disparaise or blame; nothing but well and fair And what may quiet us in a life so noble."

Today his law office, whence came so many of the eloquent dissertations and his biting criticisms, stands in a quiet byway, only a small distance removed from his grave over which daily the bells of St. Michael's send reminders of the frailty of the temporal body and the everlasting strength of great ideals.

Duelist's Ghost Is Now Quiet

The house at 76 Meeting St. is now a church rectory, but it once housed a Republican judge who laid on his son a most sorrowful epithet.

"Drunk, Drunk and a Democrat," were the words of Judge Elihu Hall Bay when his son, Andrew, a violent Democrat, was fetched home by carousing friends one night.

In addition to its political and ecclesiastical ties, the post-Revolutionary house has a ghost. This seemingly esoteric spirit hasn't appeared in the house since 1942 when it became the rectory of St. Michael's Protestant Episcopal Church next door. Whether the presence of the cloth has anything to do with it is not known.

The creature is supposedly the ectoplastic return of a young man wounded in a duel in St. Michael's Alley which runs alongside the house. He was brought into No. 76 Meeting St. and died there.

Residents prior to its occupation by the clergy reported hearing a thumping noise on the stairs, as though a limp figure was being assisted to the second floor.

The house was standing in 1785. Its exact date is not certain, but it probably was built just before that time. It is a Charleston "single house" with its wide piazzas facing the south. The street end of the porch is masked to provide an entrance door there. A wide hall transects the house and is flanked by large rooms on each side.

The main house is of cypress and pine woods from the South Carolina Lowcountry. The quaint kitchen building of locally made brick has a tiled roof. The use of brick and tile for kitchen and servants' buildings was a practice developed by the early Carolinians when they discovered the danger of fire in wooden outbuildings.

Judge Bay was a raconteur of some note and is mentioned quite often in O'Neall's "Bench and Bar of South Carolina." The incident of his son, Andrew, occurred in 1812. Judge Bay was born in Havre de Grace, Md., and began practicing law in Pensacola, Fla., where he was a king's attorney before the Revolution. He received a certificate of citizenship at Charleston Feb. 28, 1784, and bought 76 Meeting St. shortly thereafter from William Smith.

The property was listed as lot 214 on the Grand Modell of early Charleston, and lay just inside the western wall. Subsequently, it was known as the "Tan Yard" and probably played a part in the tremendous wild animal hide export business that developed in Charleston shortly after it was settled.

Judge Bay presided at the trial of Lavinia Fisher, the first woman to be hanged in South Carolina. It was he who sentenced her and her husband, John, to death in 1819 for the murder of travelers at their Six Mile House tavern. That infamous house, perhaps South Carolina's first real "tourist trap," was located near where Dorchester Road crosses the old Meeting Street Road.

On another occasion, two prisoners were brought before the judge on similar charges. One had bitten off a man's ear, the other a man's lip. The judge ordered them placed in the same cell with "permission to bite each other as much as they please."

James Jervey purchased the house from Bay in 1812 and sold it to Judge Mitchell King in 1817. In 1887 it was sold by Dr. Mitchell C. King to Langdon Cheves, Henry C. Cheves, Harriott Kinloch Barnwell and Isabel Sophia Williams as "tenants in common." They sold it to Daniel Ravenel in 1900 and he occupied it as a residence until 1942 when the vestry of St. Michael's bought it for use as a rectory.

76 Meeting — Lovely Post-Revolutionary War residence has political and ecclesiastical ties.

Property At 68 Broad Street In Same Family Since 1710

The property at 68 Broad St. may have been owned continuously by the same family line longer than any other residential tract in South Carolina.

Its (as of 1986) 276 years of continuity in the Mazyck-Ravenel lineage give it a claim to that distinction. It has been in the Ravenel family for more than 250 years and its numerous owners were all named Daniel, except for one Henry Ravenel who slipped in for a generation.

The Ravenel ownership began in 1735 when Isaac Mazyck, who got the property in 1710, left it to his daughter, Charlotte, who married Daniel Ravenel. That union joined two Huguenot families who had migrated from France after the revocation of the Edict of Nantes and sought refuge in South Carolina. The Huguenots prospered here and became major factors in econmomic, political, educational and social life of the colony and later the state.

Isaac Mazyck and Rene Ravenel arrived in Carolina in 1685. Mazyck became one of the wealthiest men in the English colonies of North America and probably South Carolina's largest landowner of his time. At his death, his holdings included Mazyck Borough, comprising the northeastern part of Charleston's peninsula area above Calhoun Street. His daughter, Charlotte, brought to the also well-to-do Daniel Ravenel a considerable dowery as well as real estate.

The residence is an amply proportioned Charleston single house with typical double front piazzas and doorway opening directly onto the street from the lower porch. It was made from brick manufactured in a Lowcountry brickyard, probably on the upper Cooper River where the Ravenels had many relatives and also plantation property.

The window lintels are of glazed brick, possibly imported from Holland since the Lowcountry kilns did not produce brick of sufficient strength to support heavy loads. These smaller brick are laid vertically at an angle with marble keystones and provide the strength necessary to carry the weight of the heavy, solid-brick, three-story walls.

Local brick, angled to the walls, form a decorative pattern under the eaves and beneath the decorative parapet masking the rise of the hip roof on the street side. Wooden dentils ornament the porch eaves. The two porches have delicately proportioned balustrades with rectangular spokes, but a decorative railing above the porch roof is much more massive and has typically curved balusters.

A narrow driveway leads to a walled garden at the rear. From the upper porch,

68 Broad — Window lintels are of glazed brick, possibly from Holland.

a view of Washington Park is afforded. It was in this park that hundreds of victims of the Charleston Earthquake of 1886 camped, and the Ravenel kitchen and other facilities were heavily taxed to assist with feeding and caring for the homeless refugees.

The mansion did not suffer materially from the earthquake. It also escaped being hit during the heavy bombardment of the city by Federal troops during the siege of Charleston in the Civil War although the spire of St. Michael's Church, immediately across Broad Street, was a reference point for the Yankee guns.

The tornado of 1939, which ripped off part of St. Michael's roof, did some damage to the Ravenel House.

It is fairly easy to date the house. The

original Mazyck residence burned in 1796 and the present house was built immediately afterward. This was during a period of great affluence in Charleston, following the Revolutionary War doldrums and prior to the economic depression caused by the break with Great Britain that resulted in the War of 1812.

The second-story drawing room of the great house is one of Charleston's loveliest salons. It has handsome cypress paneling and intricately carved mantels. From its southern end a French door leads to a balcony overlooking Broad Street. The Ravenel family probably sat here to witness the triumphal parade for the Marquis de LaFayette in 1825 when the Revolutionary War hero toured the nation to receive the thanks of a people he had risked death to aid.

45

Pink House Once Served As A Tavern

On cobbled Chalmers Street's south side stands the Pink House, a pre-Revolutionary War tavern where blue-water sailors drank grog in what was then Charleston's red light district.

Today its quaint facade hides the decorum of law offices, a half-block away from the city's legal and banking center on Broad Street. The ladies of the night long since have moved and changing transportation systems have taken the old port's piers up-harbor.

The Pink House, 17 Chalmers St., was built in the Colonial era. Recent research and discovery of an old plat indicate it could have been built in the 1694-1712 period. It was owned in 1752 by Thomas Coker, a "taverner." Its walls are of West Indian coral stone, and its tile roof is of ancient vintage.

When built, the oversized fireplace on the main floor was designed to provide heat and some means of cookery. However, the tavern probably had an outbuilding that also served as a kitchen.

In the 1930s the building had fallen into disrepair. It was rescued and restored by Mr. and Mrs. Victor B. Morawetz who added a single-story wing at the left rear so that a bathroom and kitchen might be provided without changes to the main rooms. It was bought in 1956 by Mr. and Mrs. Frank H. Bailey who added a right-rear wing flanker of one-story height, keeping the high-walled flagstoned patio with its fountain and flower beds at the rear. The two main floors were utilized as law offices and the attic as a library.

When built, the tavern was inside the locale of the original walled city of Charles Towne but outside the pale, for its street was then called Mulatto Alley and was lined with small houses, most of them bordellos. State Street (then called Union) offered similar entertainment at Chalmers east end and just across East Bay, two blocks away, the long "bridges" (finger piers) of Charleston's merchant princes jutted harborward.

Tall spars of bigantine, barkentine, schooner, sloop and man-of-war often showed against the eastern sky above the warehouses lining the "Bay," and their crews found their three "Ws" (wenches, whisky and wittles) conveniently near. From its size, the Pink House very probably was not a fashionable bistro and one finds no mention of it as a meeting place for Charleston's gentry.

Except for the durability of its construction material, the tavern probably long since would have tumbled down. Today, with its cypress paneling, narrow stairs and small-paned windows, it is much as it was more than two centuries ago.

17 Chalmers — Walls are made of West Indian coral stone.

No one knows exactly when it ceased to be a tavern and was used as a residence but this change must have occurred following the departure of the ladies of the night. This "removal" came about after 1800 when Charleston's City Council was petitioned by downtown residents to "clean up" Beresford Street, or Mulatto Alley, as the street was variously called. The bordellos found haven not too far away, in "Dutch Town," the area north of Clifford and west of King Street. They remained there until after World War II when the Navy persuaded the city to close them permanently.

In the interim, Broad Street became the legal and banking center, East Bay and Meeting the wholesale and warehouse districts. Downtown Charleston spread itself northward, gradually embracing Chalmers Street. As the area prospered, the street changed into a quiet residential area between Meeting and Church Streets, although warehouses and other commercial buildings remained between Church and State. Its inhabitants, however, were not as affluent or politically powerful as other downtown residents, a factor that probably explains why the street never was paved. Today it remains one of the few cobbled streets in the city.

Looking at the huge fireplace in the main room of the Pink House today, one easily can imagine a bright fire casting rosy light onto the sun-darkened faces of sailors as they pounded the table tops with their mugs, pinched the waitresses and recounted tales of derringdo in the earth's far corners.

And the same cobbles that today play havoc with the 20th century woman's high heels, must certainly have caused many a bruise to ale-addled seamen as they staggered out of the door of 17 Chalmers, onto mist-dampened stones and the rocky road back to the wharves.

Elfe's Shop Single House In Miniature

The elfin quality of the house at 54 Queen St. may be one of the most colossal puns ever concocted — for it was the workshop of Thomas Elfe, noted Charleston cabinetmaker.

It is a Charleston single house in miniature. Everything was scaled down to suit the taste of its builder — the ceiling heights, size of the rooms, windows, and doors. It was even built on a small lot.

Because of its perfect proportions and its pre-Revolutionary date, the house is included in the Historical American Buildings Survey. Its measurements, detailed drawings and description are filed in the National Archives along with those of such mansions as Mount Vernon, Drayton Hall and the Miles Brewton House.

Although the house is one of the city's most interesting architecturally, its probable builder and most certain user adds much to its importance.

For Thomas Elfe made furniture that was destined to grace the homes of the rich and important. Today an Elfe piece is not only a collector's dream but a very expensive item.

He collaborated with Thomas Hutchinson to make the interior woodwork for St. Michael's Protestant Episcopal Church, its communion table and the table and chairs for the South Carolina Colonial Council. The church items exist but location of the council chamber furniture is not known.

Elfe's gaminerie showed in his work for he never pasted a label on his furniture. Rather, he put so much of his obvious talent into the piece that an Elfe dresser, for instance, can fairly well be identified by a knowledgeable collector.

One distinctive Elfe motif was the fret he invariably used to decorate his better pieces of furniture and for which he charged an extra fee. The same design is found on the over-mantel of the Heyward-Washington House at 87 Church St. It is one of the remaining examples of Elfe's expert craftsmanship in house decoration as well as in cabinetry.

Another characteristic of Elfe's furniture is its interior construction. In the larger drawers of a chest he used a cross member running from front to rear at midpoint of the drawer. It is usually 1¾ inches wide, grooved on both sides and dovetailed into the front.

Sides of the drawer also are grooved. The bottoms, slightly tapered at the ends, are inserted from the rear and nailed into place. The whole makes for a tight fit without much seam showing.

Elfe used cypress mainly for the interiors of his furniture and imported large quantities of mahogany, including the Bahama mahogany, known then as "Horse Flesh" because of its bright red color.

Elfe apparently was born in London. He

54-Queen — House has an elfin quality.

came to Charleston before 1747 and fairly quickly got himself a widow as a wife, marrying Mary Hancock in 1748. She died the same year and Elfe remained a bachelor until 1755 when he married Rachel Prideau by whom he had several children. One of these became a furniture maker but moved to Savannah.

Thomas Elfe's productivity was indeed great. An account book, now in the Charleston Library Society's archives, shows that he made 1,502 pieces of furniture between 1768 and his death in 1775.

There were two houses of identical size on the lot at 54 Queen just after 1800. The one still standing has fire-scorched beams and rafters at the northern end of the roof. The fact that they are scorched on the top indicates the fire started outside. It is possible to assume that the fire of 1861, which destroyed much of the city north of this spot, burned the house on the rear of the lot and scorched the surviving one.

The property was sold in 1763 by Elfe to a chairmaker named Richard Hart. Elfe was a meticulous account keeper and a fairly generous man since his account book discloses that he gave away 50 pounds in cash one Christmas.

He also was a humane person. One of his slaves, Cato, was charged with having "feloniously and burglariously broken open the dwelling house of Lachlin Mackintosh, Esquire, and stealing sundry sums of money." Cato was found guilty and sentenced to be hanged.

Again the Elfe situation, the namesake of that most eloquent Roman being defended by Elfe, the cabinetmaker, in such a way that the court pardoned Cato.

The little house passed through many hands and reached a state of dilapidation after World War II. After one attempt was made to renovate it, it was purchased by John Francis Brenner Jr.

Mr. and Mrs. Brenner accomplished a loving bit of work in their imaginative restoration of the building. First they moved it back from the street, a happy move that gave more privacy and also provided parking spaces. Then they did a complete cleaning job on all the woodwork, uncovering the wide wainscoting and flooring in the process.

The mantel in the south room on the ground floor is a duplicate, in miniature, of the one in the Heyward-Washington House — without elaborate decorations.

The house is quite simple, two rooms up and two down with a fairly narrow hallway more reminiscent of New England hall widths than those in Charleston. The Brenners extended the rear room and attached a balcony across the back from which circular iron stairs descend to a beautiful patio of old Charleston brick. The house is operated as a museum.

The house is hard by the high wall of surrounding St. Philip's Protestant Episcopal Churchyard and a huge live oak from the cemetery stretches a limb across the patio.

'Pirate House' Name Lingers From Legends

The house at 145-147 Church St. is built of Bermuda stone, the coral basis of the island of that name, and is called the "Pirate House" because of the legend that buccaneers met there to trade with otherwise respectable Charleston merchants.

Whether the scourges of the sea actually haggled over prices inside its solid walls is unimportant. The true value of this house, and the courtyard group it joins, lies in the beauty and quaintness it lends to Charleston.

Standing almost across the street from St. Philip's Protestant Episcopal Church portico and the churchyard's high brick wall, the Pirate House group is unlike anything else in the city. And when seen while dogwood, azalea and wisteria splash color profligately next door and permeate the air with the scent of spring, the charming little houses take on a Disneyish air of unbelievability.

A very narrow walk goes from the street between the house and the churchyard wall to a paved courtyard behind the Bermuda stone building. Brick stairs lead to apartments around the court, their treads fringed with lichens that grow in the area where the sun rarely penetrates. Here, cut off from the street noises, is a quiet bit of Charleston that could have come from a motion picture set. It is one that few visitors ever see.

There is at least one other building of Bermuda stone in the city, the outbuilding at 54 South Battery. The stone generally was used for seawall and pier construction. It was brought from Bermuda as ballast in sailing ships traveling "light"

145-147 Church — Residence originally was a double house.

to Carolina to load cargo for England.

The "Pirate House" originally was a small Charleston double house with separate staircases. It was restored and converted in the late 1920s by Miss Virginia Porcher and, later, by Mrs. R. Goodwyn Rhett who completed the work.

The house was built flat on the ground, an indication it might have been constructed before Charleston builders learned that the low-lying land created damp floors unless the houses were ele-

vated above it. The exact construction date is unknown, but one may call it a pre-Revolutionary War structure with little fear of contradiction.

Its slate hip roof and an old insurance plate, issued by early 18th century insurance companies as proof of protection, all point to its antiquity.

The pirate legends could be based on fact. Merchants and others most certainly carried on traffic with pirates in most coastal towns when the Jolly Roger was well known in the sea lanes between Europe and the new world. Stede Bonnet, who was hanged at White Point Garden in 1718 and buried in the marshes near The Battery, operated along the Carolina Coast as did Blackbeard (Edward Teach), Richard Worley, Moody and others.

Charleston gave the world one of its few female pirates in Anne Bonney, illegitimate daughter of an Irish lawyer. The lawyer amassed a fortune in Charleston as a merchant and then bought a plantation hoping his daughter would marry one of the landed gentry and thus move the family into the social set.

But Anne married James Bonney, a pirate, whom she later discarded in Nassau in favor of "Calico Jack" Rackham. With him she roved the seas until 1720 when Rackham's ship was captured and its crew given typical justice in Jamaica.

Whether Anne or any other pirates ever visited the Pirate House is not definitely known, but the name persists and the legend lives on in the house from whose upper windows one may look out on the grave of Col. William Rhett, the Charlestonian who tracked Stede Bonnet down and captured him at Cape Fear.

Secluded courtyard is cut off from street noises.

Row Houses Cast A Spell Of Europe

Part of old Charleston's "difference," and one that few visitors expect, is the scattered groupings of "row houses" so familiar in Europe but relatively rare in this part of North America.

One of these colorful facades is on Queen Street, between Church and State Streets, where four of the city's more charming houses present a common front to the sightseer. Here — in 22, 24, 26 and 28 Queen St. — is a post-Revolutionary quartet that looks much as it must have more than a century and a half ago.

Their somewhat austere fronts — only one has a balcony — hide spacious rooms, beautiful woodwork and courtyards adjacent to St. Philip's Protestant Episcopal Churchyard to the north. Each has three full stories and a gable attic from which dormer windows afford views to the south and north.

Tile pots surmount the double chimneys common to each pair of houses and, when seen across the ancient headstones and brick wall of the churchyard, the houses are even more southern European in style than when seen from the street.

On the south side, garages have been placed where the original first-floor, street-front room was situated and some interior rearrangements made where modern living demanded. For the most part, however, the houses were carefully restored to their original state as much as was possible. Some have attractive brick outbuildings at the rear.

They were in terrible condition when the first restoration was undertaken in the 1940s. That section of Queen Street and most of State Street was practically a continuous slum. Across Queen Street to the south was Ryan's Barracoon, a huge, four-story brick building that originally was a barracks for slaves awaiting sale at the nearby auction sites. The Barracoon became a sort of hotel for Negroes after the sale of slaves was outlawed and planters stopping at the Planter's Hotel (now the Dock Street Theatre) put up their servants there. The Barracoon was torn down in 1950 after it was condemned as "unfit for human habitation." It housed 11 Negro families at the time.

The condition of the now-attractive row houses was not much better. In 1934, a writer described the complex — the house and wooden shacks — at 26 Queen.

He wrote: "Hot in summer, cold in winter, without modern lighting or plumbing facilities, a constant fire and health menace, it is a home for Negro families. On the line strung across the yard hangs part of the week's wash near a boiling pot in which reposes more wash. Venerable brick walls hem in the yard, shut off from the street by a three-and-a-half-story Negro tenement. the brick tenement is typi-

22-24-26-28 Queen — Former slums are now restored.

cal of many and the entire group produces an atmosphere reminiscent of residential streets in Bordeaux, France, but it is all a slum."

No. 22 Queen borders Philadelphia Alley — sometimes called "Cow Alley" — a narrow thoroughfare connecting Queen and Cumberland Streets along the rear wall of St. Philip's Churchyard.

It was in this alley that Gen. William Moultrie, en route to morning services at St. Philip's, paused long enough to satisfy a dueling challenge one Sunday. Legend has it that he "pinked" his opponent and then continued his interrupted religious trek to the church where he is reported to have sung even more lustily than was his wont.

History lives in the area — in the Huguenot Church, the Dock Street Theatre, and at St. Philip's where John C. Calhoun is buried beneath the dogwood trees. His

coffin was removed from his grave, when Charleston's fall to Union troops was imminent toward the close of the Civil War, and reburied in the churchyard immediately behind the Queen Street houses. A secret committee did the job, fearing Union soldiers might vandalize the tomb of the dead Southern leader. They reburied the coffin in the original grave after the war.

The area now is almost completely restored and is one of Charleston's fashionable residential sectors, completely different from the early days, when roistering sailors swarmed the bordellos on State and Chalmers Streets, and the later days of depressing slums. Even the names have changed. Queen formerly was Dock Street, State was Union and Chalmers, one of the last cobbled streets in Charleston, had been known as Mulatto Alley and also as Beresford Alley when it catered to the thirsts and lusts of deep-water sailors.

76-78-80 East Bay — One of America's earliest apartment houses.

Apartments Erected In 1800

Vanderhorst Row was built as a "tenement" when that word meant a respectable multiple unit dwelling.

It had deteriorated into a tenement in the modern sense before its restoration in 1936 but stands today to challenge New Orleans' Pontalba Apartments as "America's Oldest Apartment House."

Its three units — 76-78-80 East Bay — have the same space on three floors and an attic, but the central unit is somewhat more richly decorated, and has arched windows and main entrance on its street side. To the east, each of the units possesses piazzas that afford a grand view of Charleston Harbor.

The building was put up in 1800, the property of Gen. Arnoldus Vanderhorst, one-time state governor and a large landowner. It was a three-family "row house" rather than an apartment building.

Its location then was just to the harbor side of the old walled city's Curtain Line. This was a brick defense wall constructed atop the Cooper River bluff that rose above the high water mark. It ran from Market Street south to where Water Street now occupies what was originally Vanderhorst Creek.

Wharves were built between the Curtain Line and the channel by early merchants. A moat in front of the defense wall served as a general garbage dump until ordered filled by the House of Assembly. The same act (Aug. 10, 1764) prohibited construction of any buildings within 50 feet of the harbor side of the Curtain.

Petrie's map (1788) shows buildings between the wharves and East Bay Street but none in the shape of the present ones. It can be presumed that these earlier buildings were destroyed long ago but warehouses existed between Vanderhorst Row and the harbor for years, the last being torn down in 1936. The Row was restored that year by Dr. Josiah E. Smith. At that time the foundations of one warehouse were kept, forming a wall that still exists around the garden plots of the units.

A similar adjacent building, known as North Vanderhorst Row, was destroyed during the Civil War. Vanderhorst left the properties to three daughters, Hariett Horry, Marie Simons and Jane Dawson.

Following the Civil War, the building had a diversity of usages, ranging from business offices to less desirable ones. From the early 1880s until 1925, the lower floors were offices of Ravenel & Co., a cotton export firm.

North Commercial Wharf and Vanderhorst Wharf were located between the buildings and the harbor, where East Bay Playground is today. Across the street, north of 57 East Bay, stood a huge warehouse of the Commercial Cotton Press. A railroad track cut across the street at that point to serve the warehouse.

When restored, Vanderhorst Row units each contained a living room, dining room, breakfast room, butler's pantry and kitchen on the ground floor. A drawing room, bedroom, bath and piazza were on the second floor with two bedrooms and bath on the third floor and additional bedrooms, or servants' quarters, in the garrets.

The three units are occupied as single-family homes under separate ownership, a factor that probably means they face a future marked by good upkeep and little danger of again being in the center of a run-down waterfront slum.

Merchant Built Home In 1821

The mansion at 51 East Bay was the home of one of the Confederacy's most beautiful and charming belles, one of the heroines of Mary Boykin Chesnut's famous "A Diary From Dixie."

Sarah Buchanan Campbell Preston — with the preposterous name of "Buck" — came to this house as the bride of Rawlins Lowndes shortly after the Civil War. Her famous uncle, Wade Hampton, the savior of South Carolina from the evils of the Reconstruction Era, often was a guest here.

Her father-in-law, Charles Tidyman Lowndes, as one of the nation's outstanding businessmen. Twice he saved the Bank of Charleston (now the South Carolina National Bank) from collapse. The first time was during the economic panic of 1857, when he was elected temporary president, and the second was during the 1865-72 post-Civil War era when all other South Carolina banks succumbed to the disgraceful economic follies imposed by venal Reconstruction leaders.

The house has been fortunate in that it has always had good care and owners whose lives have added stature to their community. Its builder was John Fraser, an Inverness Scot who came to Charleston in 1801 and founded the great merchant house of John Fraser and Co., one of the major purveyors to the Confederate States.

The residence was bought in 1950 by Dr. and Mrs. Vince Moseley who reared nine adopted children in the house. Twenty years earlier it had been purchased by Mrs. Mary B. Parsons from Mrs. Lane Mullally, a daughter of Rawlins Lowndes. Mrs. Parsons was the widow of Edwin Parsons of New York, one of the organizers of the Southern Railway System. It was he who built the residence at The Oaks Plantation on Goose Creek that later became The Oaks Country Club house.

Mrs. Parsons, an enthusiastic gardener, recreated a beautiful garden at 51 East Bay. The Moseleys made only one change, the addition of a swimming pool.

John Fraser was one of Charleston's leading merchants when he built this house in 1821. He copied the popular Charleston single-house pattern but added dignity by constructing a spiral stairway in a wider than usual hall. The doors are of mahogany and the mantels and paneling are after the style of his fellow Scotsmen, the Adam brothers.

The main house has 15 rooms — some 22 by 22 feet. In the drawing room an Adam mantel has a palmetto tree motif while in others the Adamesque decorations are more ornate.

The drawing room has a false door — apparently added to achieve architectural balance — that opens onto an interior partition wall, a departure from the normal practice of having nonoperating doors for such purposes.

The third-floor front bedroom has a false central window, a fact that usually confuses painters to some degree.

The lower piazza and hall are floored with blue and beige tiles that are somewhat unusual in Charleston. The wide marble steps were damaged during the Civil War by artillery shelling.

In 1836 Charles Tidyman Lowndes, already a successful merchant and planter, bought the house and increased its garden by razing a house and outbuildings on Lot 49, to the south. Lowndes also added the magnificent piazzas with three differing types of classic column. They ascend in proper order, Doric, Ionic and Corinthian. He also added the garden wall.

When the banking panic of 1857 spread southward from its eastern and midwestern origins, Lowndes was asked to become temporary president of the Bank of Charleston of which he as a director. He maintained the bank's reputation for continuing specie payment despite the panic. The bank energed that year as the top discounter among the state's 20 banks.

Following the Civil War, he was made president and it was largely his genius that kept the bank solvent, the only one in the state to survive the incredibly reckless fiscal policies of the Reconstruction government.

51 East Bay — Wade Hampton was often a guest at this residence.

360 St. Margaret — The hero of San Juan Hill, Theodore Roosevelt, drank tea at this 1804 plantation house during a presidential visit to Charleston in 1902.

Generals Dueled At Lowndes Grove

Lowndes Grove, an 1804 plantation house that was built on a duel site, seems to have had an affinity for members of Congress and is one in which swashbuckling President Teddy Roosevelt attended a ladies tea — and actually drank some of the brew.

Today 360 St. Margaret St. still looks across the Ashley River marshes that haven't changed noticeably since William Lowndes built the house. But, surrounding its extensive grounds, the City of Charleston has crept in the intervening years.

The slight elevation on which the house rests was the scene of a minor skirmish in 1779 between American troops under Col. John Laurens and Hessian mercenaries of the British Army.

The plantation's first house, built prior to the Revolution about a quarter of a mile away, was burned by British troops under Gen. Augustine Prevost the same year, an act that reportedly caused its owner, John Gibbes, to die of chagrin.

The Grove also was the scene of a duel between two generals — Christopher Gadsden of South Carolina and Robert Howe of North Carolina. Gadsden and Howe initially disagreed on proposed methods for conducting the war. Then Howe was placed in charge of troops in South Carolina by the unpopular Gen. Charles Lee. Gadsden had been in command and assumed he still was. He challenged Howe's right to the command and then asked the S.C. House of Assembly to inquire as to whether Howe had ever been commissioned a general by Congress. This was not done.

Gadsden publicly charged Howe with insincerity and duplicity, words which led to the duel although seconds for both men pointed out there existed no real cause under the code duello.

Although Gadsden admitted that an apology from him would end the matter, he refused to apologize. At the Grove, he insisted that Howe fire first. The bullet nicked Gadsden's ear. He then discharged his pistol into the air before walking over to Howe and apologizing.

William Lowndes was one of South Carolina's outstanding leaders and while in Congress (1811-1822) he authored a sinking fund act that paid off the national debt in 14 years. He was speaker of the House in 1820.

The building has a one-story brick basement with black cypress weatherboarding above this level. Its handsome portico, piazza and loggia make it one of the most pleasant houses in the city.

The use of cypress wainscoting in the rooms on the main floor is an outstanding example of local artisanry at its best. Heart pine flooring and handsomely carved mantels have survived the years, and the massive front door reminds one that it was stoutly built because, in 1804 in that location outside the city, the danger of attack from Indians or brigands still remained.

The house was the scene of a tea for President Roosevelt in 1902 when he attended the S.C. Interstate and West Indian Exposition at Charleston. The city's feminine population crowded the Grove that day and many swooned when the colorful hero of San Juan Hill appeared.

The house has the unusual distinction of having been owned by a couple, both of whom were former members of Congress. It was purchased in 1937 by Albert Gallatin Simms and his wife, Mrs. Ruth Hanna McCormick Simms of Albuquerque, N.M.

Both served in the 71st Congress (1929-31) as Republicans, he from New Mexico and she from Illinois.

She was a daughter of Marcus (Mark) A. Hanna, well-known Republican "President-maker" at the turn of the century and was the widow of Medill McCormick, Chicago newspaper publisher, when she married Simms.

When they bought the house, they acquired with it an 80-year-old Negro former slave, Henry Brown, who was born on the place in 1857 and who continued to act as gardener for the Simms family until his death.

It was bought from the Simms family in 1941 by W.K. Prause of Charleston and later by Dr. Joseph Goodman.

the land was granted in 1701 to Patrick Scott who sold a portion of it to John Braithwaite in 1738. In 1769 it was in the possession of John Gibbes. In 1796 Mary Clodner, or Mary Vesey as she was known, a "free" East Indian, bought the plantation from John B. Irving to whom the Gibbes family had conveyed it. Lowndes obtained it as a result of partition suits following Mary Vesey's death.

In 1831 it was sold to Amelia, Margaret, Louisa, Anna Maria and Arthur Gordon Rose who left a complicated set of four wills, each devising the property to Arthur B. Rose who built a private track on the grounds. This is now the main drive around Hampton Park.

Rose sold it to Capt. Frederick C. Wagener of Charleston. James Sottile, a Charlestonian who later moved to Miami and amassed a fortune of more than $200 million, owned the house in the 1920s. He sold it to the Koster family from whom Simms obtained it.

631 East Bay — The Faber-Ward House was built about 1832. In former days it had an impressive view of marsh and water to the east.

Mansion Has Had A Varied Career

A gentleman's suburban villa, a planter's town house, a postbellum Negro hotel, a middle class residence, and a slum — the Faber-Ward House at 631 East Bay St. has been all of these.

Now it has been restored with its soaring Palladian portico unchanged and its "great house" image intact. For it was one of America's truly great mansions when it was built, facing the east where the Cooper and Wando rivers afforded a magnificent piece of Lowcountry scenery.

The house was built about 1832 by Henry F. Faber, a wealthy Charlestonian. The era was one during which American builders were borrowing heavily from the Italian architect, Andrea Palladio, and the Faber-Ward House was described as "unique in America" by one of Palladio's biographers, James Reynolds. In many ways it is reminiscent of the neo-classic style seen in the grand manner along the Missisippi River where prosperity permitted planters to live in baronial splendor.

Its lofty piazza pillars are set on substantial stone arches, themselves 15 feet tall, with the spaciousness and balance so typical of Palladio. Its facade could have been patterned after that of Italy's Villa Malcontenta.

Faber sold the house to Joshua Ward, a wealthy planter known around the world for the quality of his Waccamaw River long-grain rice. He also was a political fig-

ure having served as South Carolina's lieutenant-governor. The wealth of Faber and Ward was reflected in the quality of material and workmanship still evident in the mansion.

The house is believed to have contained Charleston's first non-portable bathtub.

Long-leaf yellow pine and cypress from Carolina, mahogany from the tropics, marble from Italy — these combined to provide durability to the building despite the abuse it received after the Civil War and in recent years. Each of the 12 rooms (four on each of the principal floors) had marble mantels, the stair was mahogany and plaster work and paneling were the finest that money could buy or artisans create. Silverplated pewter door handles and other examples of wealth adorned the mansion until its occupancy by Union troops after the city's fall in 1865.

Occupation officials decided it would make a grand hotel for Negroes and named it the Hamitic Hotel. Where Ward had entertained in lavish splendor, recently emancipated slaves lodged and ate. But the hotel proved a failure and the property returned to the control of whites. It was used as a family residence by the Heyward and Kingdon familes until the 1930s when it was bought by Gordon Realty Co. and converted into six apartments.

The house deteriorated gradually until the post World War II influx of poverty-

stricken rural Negroes changed the area into an almost entirely black neighborhood. Changing economic conditions took their toll of neighboring mansions that once faced the river.

In 1964 the house also seemed doomed after the Housing Authority of the City of Charleston decided to build a low-rent housing project there. The Historic Charleston Foundation saved the building by purchasing it.

A large garden once surrounded the house, but most of the land was sold. It still has a fairly large lot with two solid-brick flankers at the rear that formerly were servants' houses.

The Foundation sold the property to Arthur Ravenel Jr., who restored the main building as an office and three large apartments. The two outbuildings also were restored as rental units.

Visitors arriving in Charleston from the East Cooper area get a beautiful view of the house from the bridges, its symmetry and style making it stand tall and proud above its more prosaic neighbors.

The harbor still may be seen from its hexagonal cupola but the wide marshes and winding creeks that once came up to its lordly portico are now filled with railroad tracks, waterfront piers and business establishments. Above them, the old house looms as a symbol of an era when Charleston was the queen of all Southern cities and rice was king.

Seven Rental Houses Supported This Elizabeth Street Mansion

Of the "Seven Days of the Week" that once supported the "big house" at 48 Elizabeth St., only two remain and they no longer maintain the mansion in the style it once knew.

The house looks southward, down Elizabeth, from behind its long piazzas. The entrance is on the west where a huge wood, iron and glass door swings wide to disclose one of the most elegant white marble foyers and stairways in America.

From this door antebellum occupants could look westward along Wragg Mall at the "Seven Days in the Week." These were seven substantial Charleston double houses. They were built as rental units by Gov. William Aiken and each was supposed to bring in enough revenue to pay for one day's maintenance of the mansion.

Five of the houses were torn down after World War II to make room for an enlargement of Courtenay Public School. Each was quite large and provided with a big lot and servants' quarters. One family rented one of the houses from the day it was completed until it was demolished more than 100 years later. It was estimated that they had paid more than 10 times the value of the house during that time.

The mansion was built in the 1817 for John Robertson and purchased by William Aiken in 1826. Aiken was owner of substantial plantation lands and lived in the grand manner. Construction of the "Seven Days" is ample proof of not only his affluence but his business acumen as well.

Flanking Wragg Mall, the houses were situated in what was then one of the more fashionable sections of the city. Today the area has deteriorated and the Aiken House was one of the last of the huge mansions to be owned and occupied by descendants of the antebellum proprietors.

Mrs. I'On Rhett, widow of a direct descendant of Gov. Aiken, occupied the mansion until 1972. In 1975 the property was donated to the Charleston Museum for restoration as a house museum.

The house has fairly simple woodwork in its large rooms but has magnificent chandeliers under which Jefferson Davis walked when he was a guest of the Aikens in 1863. As president of the Confederate States, Davis was on an official visit to Charleston at the time. It is realistic to assume that he rode in one of the two existing antebellum carriages that were kept in the carriage house flanker along Elizabeth Street at the rear of the mansion.

Across the paved courtyard on the east side of the lot is another brick flanker that included a kitchen and servants' quarters.

The lot runs all the way through the block to Mary Street at the north and has magnificent magnolia trees. The rear lot is secluded behind high brick walls. In the northeast and northwest corners are "necessaries" with louvered gothic doors and windows, built triangular-shaped into the corners.

The former stables in the carriage house still have the original wooden feed racks which clearly show the gouges caused by over-eager horses as they chewed at hay in the slatted troughs.

Between the front (south side) of the house and Judith Street is a small garden in front of the basement arches that support the double-tiered piazzas.

High above the garden, basement and piazzas, the third floor of the house opens its windows above the porch roof. A double window, centered, is flanked by two single windows on each side of this floor while above a gabled roof has a "half bull's eye" for ventilation of the garret.

The Aiken House is one of the Charleston's largest residences, a factor that recommended it to Gen. P.G.T. Beauregard when Federal shelling of the lower part of the city forced removal of his headquarters to a safer location. He occupied the house from the end of 1863 until he left the city in April 1864.

Community Saved House From Ruin

Individuals, a society, an entire community, a state and, finally, a nation had a hand in saving the Joseph Manigault House from destruction.

Today the 350 Meeting St. mansion is recognized as one of the most perfect Adam-style houses in America.

It also has a hidden stairway between second and third floors, lovely furniture and a garden of the style popular when the house was built in 1803.

However, contrary to local legend, it does not have an underground passageway to the Cooper River.

The house is owned by the Charleston Museum. It is operated as a museum and is open to visitors.

Aside from its architectural importance, it is filled with exceptionally beautiful furnishings, paintings and relics of the years during which it was occupied as the town house of one of South Carolina's wealthiest planters.

It was Joseph Manigault's brother, Gabriel, who designed the house in the pattern of a great parallelogram. Its right-angled severity is broken pleasingly by a stairwell bow on the north wall, a bowed piazza to the west and offset wide porches on the south where the formal garden affords a pleasant view toward the attractive domed gatehouse.

The area was known as Wraggboro and Joseph Manigault's mother was Elizabeth Wragg whose family provided the large lot fronting on Meeting and bounded north and south by John Street and Ashmead Place.

The house had fallen on hard times when the long battle to save it began in 1920. It was then a boarding house and in bad state of repair but structurally still sound. This was in part due to Manigault's integrity as a builder. The wooden porch pillars, for instance, are on stone plinths to prevent rot. Between sub-floor and heart-pine flooring, a layer of lime was laid to discourage insects. Behind each baseboard, where normally a space exists, an extra layer of brick was cemented, preventing the normal use of the space as a rat and roach thoroughfare.

The slate roof lies atop heavy pine rafters, all carefully pegged together.

In 1920, endangered by threats of demolition, the house was saved temporarily by being purchased and then having the garden area sold to an oil company. A service station was built in the garden and the gatehouse became a storage area.

The Society for the Preservation of Old Dwellings (now the Charleston Preservation Society) came into the battle. In 1933 an anonymous donor bought the house and gave it to the museum. Two years later the oil company gave the service station site to the museum. The Charleston Garden Club joined the fight, and "Yankee" winter residents of the Lowcountry got interested

350 Meeting — The Joseph Manigault House.

and restoration began.

Fortunately, the formal garden design had been traced by Charleston Architect Albert Simons in 1916 and that design was reincorporated into the garden when it was restored after World War II. During the war, the United Service Organization (USO) used the house as a women's club, and the museum began detailed restoration after the USO moved out.

When the old house was assured of restoration in 1935, it attracted nationwide attention. The dean of the Harvard School of Architecture offered assistance. The F.P. Garvans, winter residents of Yeaman's Hall, donated 100,000 "Charleston" brick that had come from demolished buildings in the city.

The intricate ceiling over the stairway had been restored in 1930 by Mrs. Francis B. Crowningshield of Boston. Gifts came from many places — English porcelain, Leeds pottery, Waterford glass, Canton chinaware, satinwood bookcases, Louis XV and XVI furniture — all in keeping with the magnificence and style of the mansion.

Portraits of Joseph Manigault and his parents, Peter and Elizabeth, are on display along with other Manigault paintings. That of Peter Manigault is a copy of an oil by Alan Ramsay. Elizabeth Manigault's portrait was painted in 1757 by Jeremiah Theus. Some were twice rescued, once following the Civil War when family members found them ripped from their frames and nailed to the walls of former slave quarters at one of the Manigault plantations and again when discovered in the attic of the old mansion where children had vandalized them.

Today the old house is much as it was in its heyday as a home. Small areas of

The Gatehouse.

woodwork and plaster were left unpainted to show the original colors, and visitors may view the hidden stairs leading between partition walls from the second floor east hall to the third floor west hall.

Each Christmas the Manigault House is decorated by the Garden Club of Charleston and from its windows the glow of candlelight reflects across the lawn of the old Second Presbyterian Church to the south and onto what is left of the Old Citadel to the west.

It is one of the great houses, built in what was then a suburb, that has survived the double onslaught of "progress" prior to World War II and slum encroachment following the war.

Residence Saw Birth Of Historic Railroad

Eagle adorns hall ceiling.

The house at 456 King St. was the home of the president of the company that built America's first steam engine railroad for freight and passengers, and it probably was in the original parlor that the railroad had its conception.

The S.C. Canal and Railroad Co. built the line over which the "Best Friend" pulled cars as far west as Hamburg, S.C., just opposite Augusta, Ga. When completed in 1834 it was the longest railroad in the world. Part of the original roadbed still carries trains past the high brick wall at rear of the house.

The original firm eventually became part of the Southern Railway System and the house was used for offices. In 1977 the National Trust for Historic Preservation established southern regional offices in the building and two years later Southern donated the house to that organization retaining office space on a rental basis.

The original house consisted of the portion immediately at the southeast corner of King and Ann Streets. The remainder was added by the Aiken family. The original portion appears to have been built between 1807 and 1811. In 1807 William Smith, acting as trustee for James Mackie, a minor, bought the lot for $3,495. William Aiken bought the property four years later from Mackie's executors for $14,000, the increase in price indicating that a building had been constructed in the interim. In addition, comparison of the mahogany stair rail and accompanying wainscoting with other definitely dated houses places it in that period.

Aiken was an Irish immigrant who made a fortune as a Charleston merchant. He married Henrietta Wyatt of Charleston. Their son, William Aiken Jr., became state governor and a congressman. He lived in this house from boyhood until he established himself in a mansion two blocks away at 48 Elizabeth St.

The senior Aiken and other leading citizens of Charleston reportedly met in his home to plan formation of the famous railroad. Aiken, however, never lived to see it completed. The line ran only as far as the Six Mile House (near North Charleston's Reynolds Avenue) when Aiken died. His death in March 1831 was ironical. The father of S.C. railroading died from injuries received when his carriage horse ran away, overturning the vehicle.

The older portion of the house is in the Adam tradition and contains rich wood and stucco ornamentation. A huge plaster "spread eagle" bearing a cluster of grapes in its beak looks down from the ceiling at the top of the stairwell. Elaborate rosettes adorn the first and second floor hall ceilings and a quite elaborately decorated doorway, with fanlight, sidelights and columns, leads from the hall to the piazza on the second floor.

The street-front room on the second story has two handsome doors. The one connecting to the hall is skillfully contrived to appear as a single-leaf door but is made of two vertical sections, hinged in the center. On the same wall is a matching false door, placed there to obtain the Adam symmetry.

Aiken's widow married George Edwards, a planter. The 1837-38 city directory lists 456 King St. as his residence. Either Mrs. Edwards or her son, Gov. Aiken, added the Victorian-styled octagonal wing with its very handsome second-story ballroom where elaborate ceiling ornaments and tall windows lend elegance. This wing was damaged in the 1886 earthquake and was so trussed in by iron bands and bolts that Charlestonians said it appeared to be wearing a corset.

In 1863 Gov. Aiken sold the house to the South Carolina and Georgia Railroad Co. for $50,000 (probably Confederate money). It came into possession of the Southern Railway in 1899. The house's servants' wing is intact and a gothic-style coach house still stands at the eastern end of the extensive gardens.

Woodwork, mantel and putty ornamentations from the first-floor front room were taken out in 1930 and removed to Washington where they were used to decorate Southern Railway's presidential office. Massive wrought iron gates and fencing were presented to the Carolina Art Association. They stand today in Gateway Walk between the Gibbes Art Gallery and the Charleston Library Society.

A pleasant aspect of the house is the clever use of wide piazzas, in the Greek revival style, to join the Adam and Victorian sections into an illusion of unity.

The two styles, each having been taken at the peak of the popularity of their diverse characteristics, represent much of the best in Charleston building and reflect the excellent tastes of members of one of South Carolina's notable families.

456 King — Wide piazzas blend Adam and Victorian styles of architecture into a harmonious unit.

Builder Of Mansion Helped Build Nation

First in war, first in education and first in religion — so might be described the builder of the Georgian mansion at 6 Glebe St.

For in its basement were held the first classes of the College of Charleston; down its sandstone steps strode the English-born rector of the Anglican Church of St. Philip's to announce to his congregation that he was doffing his surplice and donning a revolutionist's military uniform, and back to its high-ceiled, cypress-panelled rooms came a Revolutionary War hero to be named the first bishop of the state he had helped to create.

He was Robert Smith and today the magnificent house he built in 1770 is known as the Bishop Smith House, home of the presidents of the College of Charleston. The year the house was built was the same year the College of Charleston Endowment was established and only the intervening war of the Revolution delayed the college's chartering, an event recorded by the State of South Carolina in 1785.

The house was known for years as "Glebe House," taking its name from the lands it occupied, lands left to St. Philip's Protestant Episcopal Church by Affra Coming to be used as income producing rentals.

The house on Glebe Street once occupied a lot extending south to Wentworth, east to St. Philip, north to George and West to Coming Street. Gradually the surrounding area was sold off by the church, but the three-story-and-garret residence still dominates the neighborhood, standing as tall, square and solid as the day it was completed.

But it was not always so. The house ceased being a permanent rectory when Bishop Smith died in the early 1800s, and the church rented it out. It had deteriorated to the status of a run-down apartment house when the College of Charleston bought it in 1961. Part of the funds for its purchase were donated by three of the bishop's descendants, W. Mason Smith, W. Mason Smith Jr. and J.J. Pringle Smith. They, and other descendants, subsequently gave a substantial portion of the large amount needed to renovate the building and render it habitable as a 20th century residence.

Fortunately, the interior had not been changed materially. The floor-to-ceiling cypress paneling was intact and only the plaster, nearly 200 years old, had to be completely replaced. The house is a typical Charleston double house with four main rooms to a floor and a very large central hallway.

The front door originally did not have the present wood frame and pediment but consisted of a simple brick opening with a fanlight above the massive heart-pine door. Apparently the trim was added after 1900 and the restorers felt it was more in

Network of roof supports.

keeping with the grand style of the house to install a similar one than to revert to the more simple entrance decor.

The only major changes made in the house were formation of a library in the northwest rear room of the main floor, use of the entire front half of the basement as a ballroom and the installation of modern plumbing. All was accomplished without disturbing the style or proportions of the interiors.

The four front rooms have floor-to-ceiling cypress paneling made of unusually wide boards. One of the hand-carved panels is 42 inches wide.

Restoration of the house was a major project of Dr. George D. Grice who retired in 1968 as president of the college.

Mrs. Bushrod B. Howard and Mrs. Lionel K. Legge acted as volunteer supervisors for the restoration work that was done by Herbert DeCosta.

The wrought iron gates are new and were designed by Samuel G. Stoney using as a basic pattern the west gates of St. Philip's Church and incorprating a bishop's miter and crossed croziers.

The Bishop Smith House was included among those selected for measurement and drawing by the Historic American Building Survey and its exact details are on file in the National Archives. Throughout the house, the restorers uncovered evidence of the permanency intended by its builder. Its thick walls, of old Charleston brick, combine with heart-pine sills and huge risers to support the massive roof. In the attic, details of the intricately-planned support system are visible today. The attic is reached by a spiral stair, steep and narrow but fitting nicely between one of the major chimneys and the hall.

The college has restored the garden and preserved the old "tabbywork" cistern near the front steps. This old tank stored rainwater from the roof in the days before the city water system existed.

6 Glebe — The Bishop Smith House was built in 1770.

House Recalls City's Golden Age

18 Bull — When constructed, this magnificent residence looked across the marshes of Coming's Creek.

In 1800 one could sit on the broad northside piazzas of the house at 18 Bull St. and admire a typically Lowcountry view across the marshes of Coming's Creek just beyond the formal gardens.

Today a brick wall blocks only a part of the modern hodgepodge beyond. The creek long since was filled and built upon, its winding marsh banks replaced by the harsher rectangular outlines of streets.

But the old house is much the same, presenting its handsome facade to the street, hiding its piazzas behind its massive bulk and, externally at least, is a fine example of the prosperous times it represents.

It was built during one of the most fruitful eras of Charleston, that period from about 1790 until the War of 1812 slowed the flood of commerce that brought the city wealth.

William Blacklock, the builder, was a member of the board of the Branch Bank of the United States in Charleston. He signed the notice asking for bids on the bank's building (now Charleston's City Hall) the same year he was having his own substantial suburban villa constructed on Bull Street in Harleston Village.

It is a massive house set back from the sidewalk just the width of the matched front stairs that are supported by marble columns surrounding a basement entry. Seen from across the street, the wrought iron railings form a stark black pattern across the white front door. The door is solidly placed in a frame of intricately designed sidelights and is topped by one of the city's handsomest fanlights. The entry is set is a wide brick arch that is flanked on either side by narrower window arches.

A wide rectangular window on the second floor lacks the contrasting brick headers with their contrasting inset keystones. The low arch of the main door is complemented by a wide-flung fanlight in the attic gable four stories above the ground.

The old Charleston brick in the main house undoubtedly were baked on one of the Lowcountry rivers. Heart pine sills and flooring came from the once plentiful longleaf pines inland and cypress paneling was a product of Lowcountry swamps.

Wooden gates formerly hung in the wide driveway and at the pedestrian walks on either side of the house. At the rear, overlooking the garden, is a quaint Gothic outbuilding, now a rental unit, and a smaller brick unit, also converted into an apartment.

The house was owned in 1821 by William Clarkson and subsequently passed through many hands. Just prior to World War I, the German consul at Charleston, E.H. Jahnz, owned it but the break with Germany took away his consular status. By 1921 it had changed hands again, was occupied as a boarding house for about 12 years and, in 1936, became the home of a Phi Chi fraternity of the Medical College, now the Medical University of South Carolina.

E. des Brosses Hunter purchased the house in 1937 and restored it to its former magnificence. Following World War II, his son converted the residence into an apartment complex. The second floor became a single unit while the basement and first floor each accommodated two apartments.

In 1950 the building was sold to Dr. Maxcy C. Harrelson Jr. who sold it in 1968 to Richard H. Jenrette, a Wall Street stock broker who has restored several Charleston buildings.

Jenrette donated the Blacklock House to the College of Charleston for use as an alumni house.

Except for the basement units, the entire main house is now used by alumni and faculty. In addition to regular dining facilities, group meetings and dinners are held in the building.

The house has an unusually large lot, a factor which makes it attractive as a potential parking area in a section where parking is at a premium. Preservationists in past years have expressed fear that it might be lost in this manner or be torn down to provide a site for some other form of construction. However, the surrounding area has been restored in recent years and the future of the house seems secure.

This is one of Charleston's truly magnificent pieces of architecture as well as one of the largest residences in the city. It is listed as nationally important in the book: "This is Charleston."

Ashley Hall Formerly Housed Confederate States Treasurer

One of the more interesting and architecturally pleasing buildings in Charleston is the former residence at 172 Rutledge Ave. that now is the administrative building of Ashley Hall School.

The original portions of the old mansion date to the 1815-1825 period when Regency was the fashionable style in architecture and furniture.

The house became a school in 1909 and remains today one of the better preparatory institutions in the country.

Prior to its debut in the academic world, the mansion was lived in by some of the leading families of the Charleston area. The owners include a foreign consul, an internationally known banker and cotton broker who became treasurer of the Confederate States of America, a wealthy Scotch-Irish businessman and a planter.

Patrick Duncan was the first owner of record and his house, built with income from a tallow chandlering business and profits from real estate, was in the suburban area outside Cannonsborough.

Duncan bought the house site in 1798 from Daniel Cannon and, in 1807, added a lot to the south.

He sold the property to James Nicholson in 1829. George A. Trenholm acquired the place later and was living there during the Civil War. After Trenholm's death in 1877, Charles Otto Witte, banker and German consul, bought it.

Trenholm generally is regarded as the single most effective person in the Confederacy insofar as economic relations with Europe were concerned. He was senior partner in the John Fraser Co., one of the largest handlers of Sea Island long-staple cotton, a firm with strong financial ties in England and Europe.

At the onset of war, Trenholm personally financed the outfitting of 12 small coastal defense ships for the Confederate Navy.

Through a Fraser connection in Liverpool, some 60 blockade runners were outfitted and these ships were the mainstay of the Confederacy on imported goods, such as medicine, which the Union forces had embargoed.

Witte, who made a fortune in two banks, had been named consul for the Free State of Hamburg in 1855 and then became consul for the North German Federation of States. After the Franco-Prussian War, the German Empire was formed and Witte became its consul. He resigned in 1907.

The name of the architect who designed the house is not certain but it probably was William Jay who worked in Charleston and Savannah, Ga. after 1817. The architecture of the structure strongly resembles houses in Savannah that are known to have been designed by Jay.

His designs are identifiable because of his wide use of an exuberant range of ar-

172 Rutledge — Portico columns spaced to give open view of entrance.

chitectural detail in the Regency style. The soaring eliptical stairway, curved walls, rounded door and window heads, curved doors, grandiose portico and rounded balconies in the house here all have the Jay touch.

The soaring portico at Ashley Hall has four ionic columns that are not placed as usual but two to a side, a plan that gives an open view of the winding iron balcony rails and the huge door opening into the second floor.

This is typical of Jay and so is the exterior work on the basement, through which a wide hall leads to the first stairway. The basement walls are reticulated, the deeply

beveled blocks forming interesting patterns around the arched window and door openings.

Jay's use of the Gothic style also is evident in the over-portico windows on the fourth floor and in the vaulted interior ceilings.

From the basement, the staircase mounts in eliptical curves to the fourth floor. The stairway has spiral terminals, mahogany handrails, slender balusters and decorative spandrels and fretwork.

The house has been named the McBee House in honor of Mary Vardrine McBee, founder of the school.

101 Rutledge — Newspaper editor was slain in basement of this house.

Residence Was Scene Of Sensational Slaying

The "eyebrows" over the windows of the house at 101 Rutledge Ave. cast heavy shadows on the windows, giving the house a demure look that belies its role in the city's most sensational murder case.

For in its basement the editor of The News and Courier, Capt. F. Warrington Dawson, was shot to death about 4:20 p.m. March 10, 1889, by a young physician.

The story had just about everything to give it sensationalism. The three principals were Capt. Dawson, his children's 22-year-old French-speaking Swiss governess, Marie Burdayron, and 30-year-old Dr. Thomas Ballard McDow.

Capt. Dawson lived just around the corner on Bull Street in an elaborate mansion. Dr. McDow had recently come to Charleston. A native of Lancaster, S.C., he had previously practiced in upper South Carolina and Georgia. He was married to a German woman who came equipped with a fairly handsome dowry.

Dr. McDow maintained his offices in the basement of 101 Rutledge and lived upstairs. Marie Burdayron was to testify at the trial that the handsome young doctor first propositioned her on Feb. 1, 1889.

She stated that McDow gave her a gold watch and a novel "Twixt Love and Law," a Victorian tale of a married man's passion for a single girl.

She also admitted going to a Negro house on Cannon Street with McDow, testimony that threw the crowded court room into laughter.

McDow's lawyer asked her: "Why did he take you there? Did you think he wanted to play croquet with you?"

Speaking in broken English, Marie answered: "Oh, no, not that." Then she asked the lawyer: "M'sieu, suppose we talk in French awhile." The News and Courier account stated that Marie then left the stand, passing close to McDow and "he moved his chair to let her go by and hung his head and two thousand pairs of eyes were on them both."

From the time a "groundnut" (peanut) woman sounded the alarm, to the jury's verdict June 30, 1889, Charleston was in an uproar. The case was a partisan affair. Capt. Dawson, an Englishman who fought with the Confederacy, had combined the Charleston Courier and The Daily News to form the News and Courier in 1872. He was a powerful force in the community but not popular with the masses. McDow, a newcomer, and practically unknown, overnight became the symbol of the "little man" fighting the status quo.

He was small in physique and Dawson was a powerful, large man. There also was speculation that Dawson's "fatherly" interest in his children's pretty young governess might cover a deeper feeling. The Victorian age's double standard still prevailed and the doctor's dalliance with the governess might have carried no great social onus until it became published news.

McDow testified that Dawson, whom he had never met although their back yards almost butted, came to his office, threatened him with public denouncement and then attacked him with his cane. The doctor said he had been forced down on a couch and was being badly battered when he drew a pistol from his hip pocket and fired once.

The doctor tried to bury Dawson's body under the floor boards of a basement closet and it was three hours after the fatal shot that he went outside and told a policeman he had killed Dawson.

The trial attracted the largest crowds ever to attend a court hearing in Charleston. When the jury announced its verdict of innocent, the audience broke into cheers and continued cheering until the judge threatened to jail them all on contempt charges.

The unanimous verdict attracted strong partisan editorials locally and in out-of-town newspapers. The Savannah paper theorized that the jury (seven blacks and five whites) had destroyed a Negro argument that white juries would not convict whites but would convict blacks. The paper stated that the predominantly Negro jury had been given a chance to convict a white man and had failed.

The house itself is a typical antebellum Charleston single house of solid brick without pretension, although its eaves are undergirt by slightly fancy brickwork and the heavy overwindow "eyebrows" are in three styles. The wood decorations on the ends of the porches are late Victorian.

The house has a large garden with a particularly handsome palmetto tree and shrubs.

The house was purchased about 1926 by J.C. Elson who restored it. After World War II it was purchased from the Elson family by Mr. and Mrs. Edward P. Holcombe III and later was owned by Dr. and Mrs. Thomas L. Lucas and their son, Dr. Thomas L. Lucas Jr. of Anderson. They rented it as two units, one in the coach-house at rear and the other in the main dwelling.

94 Rutledge — Town house of wealthy Sea Island cotton planter is a reflection of elegance.

Planter Built House In 1854

The full sophistication of antebellum Southern "Society" permeates the feeling imparted by the residence at 94 Rutledge Ave.

For this is "Country Come to Town" in the elegant sense of the phrase — the "country" being that of the antebellum "Gone With the Wind" era.

Its magnificence reflects the wealth of the Sea Island cotton planter whose empire reached its zenith coincident with the fires of sectionalism that were to destroy it and the society it created. The dwelling was the town house of Isaac Jenkins Mikell of Peter's Point Plantation, Edisto Island.

The Peter's Point house, while commodious, comfortable and scenic, lacks the refinements of architectural taste that Mikell lavished on 94 Rutledge Ave. The big house on the plantation commands the Edisto River with the islands and sweep of St. Helena Sound beyond. The site is one of the most beautiful in the Lowcountry.

Mikell's town house could sit "at ease" on Peter's Point for its monumental Corinthian portico would have allowed its owners a much-romanticized "Southern" backdrop from which to view the glories of the tidewater country. This house is, indeed, the prototype of Margaret Mitchell's "Tara" in a metropolitan setting.

Its designers kept the illusion of a spa-

cious woodland setting by providing a formal garden before its capacious porch. Beyond the garden tall magnolia trees form a solid bank of greenery that cuts off the mundane city sights beyond. Within the garden, formal hedges and floral beds established a sylvan environment that (before the era of the automobile) provided serenity reminiscent of Edisto.

That serenity Mikell could well afford. In addition to Peter's Point, he owned and operated two other Sea Island cotton plantations. In his life — rich, full, vigorous, romantic — Mikell was the human parallel of the virtues of the long-staple cotton that made it all possible.

He was born less than 20 years after the production of long-fibered cotton was established on the Sea Islands, about 1790, and his death (1881) was not four decades removed from the advent of the boll weevil which effectively killed the long cotton business during World War I.

Mikell included in his town house some of the "grandeur that was Greece, the glory that was Rome," and it was truly a labor of love. The house was built for his third wife whom he was to describe later as the love of his life. The Rutledge Avenue house was built in 1854 when Mikell was 46 years old.

In his old age, he reminisced that he scarcely remembered his first bride; his second brought him success and wealth,

the third was the "love of my life" and the fourth marriage, in 1864, provided comfort in his old age.

His town house also captured something typically "Charleston" in its use of an end of the house as the main entrance. Through marble-paved halls, one enters the huge foyer that backs up the portico and is the focal point of the residence. From it, stairs curve upward and tall porch doors open onto the garden.

On a moonlit night, with a mocking bird singing beyond the balustraded veranda, all that is needed is for Scarlet O'Hara to come swooping down the stairs. Margaret Mitchell wrote about it, Hollywood immortalized it on film, but an Edisto Island planter had it all well in hand a hundred years earlier.

The house has large grounds that included a service wing and carriage house. Today the house has been restored and divided into spacious units. It faced almost certain destruction in 1962 when Charleston County abandoned it as a public library.

Mr. and Mrs. Charles H. Woodward of Philadelphia and Charleston bought and renovated the house with very little alteration of its original design. They have provided handsome apartments, two in the main section, one at the rear of the service wing and one in the former carriage house.

Traditional Southern House Overlooked Owner's Rice Mill

No. 172 Tradd St. was built by a bachelor and during its early years missed matrimony, a major fire and the ravages of war.

It also is one of the few existing relics of the era when this part of the South began to build this type of traditionally Southern house.

However, its builder was not stingy, and the probable architect, a German, was true to his eclectic training in planning the house. He borrowed heavily from the Corinthian order in the Choragic Monument to Lysicrates for the majestic portico.

Here are found skillfully carved wooden imitations of the Greek forerunner. Artisans shaped tendrilled volutes, flowerettes and foliage for the capitals, and the whole is one of majestic simplicity, tastefully ornamented.

When Alexander Hext Chisolm built this house in 1836, the site gave it superintendency over his rice mill to the west and it

guarded the causeway that extended from the end of Tradd Street to the mill. The Ashley River marshes permitted an unhampered view of the river and lower harbor.

To its west, a huge mill pond stored tidal water between Broad Street (extended) to the north, Rutledge Avenue to the east and the slight rise to the west upon which Chisolm's Mill stood. The site of the mill house is about where the workshop of the U.S. Coast Guard base stands today.

Thus it is a reminder of the glory of the Greek revival in architecture. It also was a commercial mill complex of the type that was beginning to change the Southern area of the nation from completely agricultural to somewhat industrial when the Civil War intervened.

Its lot was part of one of the major antebellum expansions of the city. Both Tradd and Broad Streets petered out in the salt marshes near the present site of New

Street and it was to the marshes south of Tradd and west of New that entrepreneurs looked for new lands on which to build.

The first power units in the city were built along its westerly river bastion in the form of windmills. These were patterned after those of the Netherlands and used to power rice mills, grist mills and even sawmills before the days of tidal-water power and steam.

The development began in 1817 when Joshua Brown purchased from city council the area extending westerly from New Street between Broad and Tradd Streets. He made a millpond there and sold the entire property to John Duncan in 1819. Duncan operated a sawmill with tidewater power until a fire destroyed his buildings in 1826.

The Chisolm family bought him out in 1829, rebuilt the sawmill and added a rice pounding machine. This gave the industrial complex year-round work, a very agreeable arrangement since rice hulling was primarily an autumnal task.

The advent of steam made the pond less necessary for functional operation of the mill and the Chisolms began filling it with rice chaff and sawdust, a task that continued until well after the end of the 19th century.

The architect probably was Charles F. Reichardt. It was he who had placed the soaring colonnade on the now destroyed Charleston Hotel to make it one of America's most attractive hostelries of the day.

Reichardt adapted the Greek Cross for the layout of the house with the portico as one, somewhat blunted, arm to the south. The north wing, housing the smaller rooms, formed the other arm. The major rooms, extending east and west, completed the axis.

The huge entrance door, centered under the portico, opens directly into a large stair hall. The stairs spiral gracefully up a semicircular wall, affording a gentle rise and requiring none of the bulky landings found in so many houses.

The doors are of heart pine with a single panel and are about three inches thick. Their heaviness is relieved through use of white porcelain knobs decorated with gaily colored sprigs of tiny flowers.

Chisolm sold the house to William A. Alston of All Saints Parish in 1855. Sometime later the northern arm of the cross was filled in to provide more room. The Alstons occupied the dwelling until 1924 as a town house and as a permanent residence when rice failed as a staple crop on the coast.

From 1924 until 1940 it was the home of Frederick Richards. Peter Samuel Bee maintained it as his residence from 1940 until 1966 when it was bought by A. Rhett duPont who renovated and restored it.

172 Tradd — Architect designed residence in the form of a Greek Cross.